Unapologetically Me

Unapologetically Me

TALES FROM
MY PERFECTLY
IMPERFECT
LIFE

BREE TOMASEL
with Sophie Neville

ALLEN&UNWIN
AUCKLAND·SYDNEY·MELBOURNE·LONDON

FOR THOSE LIVING AUTHENTICALLY AS THEMSELVES,
AND THE ONES STILL SEARCHING FOR THE COURAGE.
BE YOU, BE FREE.

Some names, places and identifying details have been
changed to protect the identify of the individuals.

First published in 2024

Text © Bree Tomasel
Images © author's personal collection

All rights reserved. No part of this book may be reproduced or transmitted
in any form or by any means, electronic or mechanical, including
photocopying, recording or by any information storage and retrieval
system, without prior permission in writing from the publisher.

Allen & Unwin
Level 2, 10 College Hill, Freemans Bay
Auckland 1011, New Zealand
Phone: (64 9) 377 3800
Email: auckland@allenandunwin.com
Web: www.allenandunwin.co.nz

83 Alexander Street
Crows Nest NSW 2065, Australia
Phone: (61 2) 8425 0100

A catalogue record for this book is available from
the National Library of New Zealand.

ISBN 978 1 991006 75 2
Design by Megan van Staden
Cover photo by Michelle Hyslop
Clothing suppliers: Blue denim shirt and jeans by Marle
Jewellery by Lindi Kingi Jewellery

Set in Tiempos
Printed and bound in Australia by the Opus Group

10 9 8 7 6 5 4 3 2 1

MIX
Paper | Supporting
responsible forestry
FSC® C001695

Contents

INTRODUCTION	9
OH, BRIANNA!	16
WOGGY-STYLE	27
TERROR	38
TOMBOY TOMASEL	52
RIDING THE CRIMSON WAVE	65
SO LONG, STANTHORPE	72
I KISSED A GIRL (AND I LIKED IT)	86
THE BEAT GOES ON	95
LESBIAN-ISH	109
MENTY-B #1	118
PRIDE	129
GAY PANIC	139
A LEAP OF FAITH	148
DO YOU LIKE MATHS?	170
LITTLE TERRAMOTO	182
TWO LITTLE MICE	201
WHITNEY HOUSTON AND MERYL STREEP	219
MENTY-B #2	227
THE GREAT SPERM HUNT	240
TO BE CONTINUED . . .	255
ACKNOWLEDGEMENTS	263

Introduction

I know what you're thinking — why the fuck has Bree Tomasel written a book? It's a valid question and one I've asked myself many times over the past year.

When I was first asked to do this, I thought it was a joke. Me, write a book? HA!

I had to (shamefully) admit to Michelle, the kindest, most patient publisher whose job it was to get me to agree to this bonkers idea, that given I'd never managed to read a book from start to finish, it was unlikely I'd be able to write one.

'I don't have the attention span,' I told her. 'I'm not interesting enough.' 'Who would want to read about me?' The reasons not to do it were endless.

She brushed my concerns off. 'You'll be fine.' 'It'll be great.' 'Just believe in yourself.' Positive encouragement flowed out of this woman with ease. She talked about writing books like it was a normal thing for people to do. 'It'll be easy once you get going.'

She obviously didn't know me very well. I am actually quite useless. I put things off. I can't focus. I panic. I lose sleep. 'I am not the sort of person who can write a book,' I tell her. 'I have ADHD, for god's sake!' But she won't give up.

I ring my parents and tell them I've been asked to write a book.

'What about?' they enquire, unable to hide their amusement at the idea of their farting, swearing daughter, the one who only just scraped through uni, sitting still for long enough to write a book. 'Um, it's a book about me.'

They laugh loudly down the phone. 'It's not a joke,' I point out. They keep laughing.

I put it out of my mind for a while. I ignore emails and screen calls, because that's my super-power. I push it so far out of my mind I can almost pretend it's not happening. But something weird happens without me really realising it. The concept of sharing my stories settles somewhere in my brain and starts growing like a little seed. Suddenly, ideas for what I could write about are sprouting like little leaves. Maybe I *could* write a book? Maybe there are people out there who would like some of my stories? Hell, maybe they'd even benefit from them?

'Okay, I'll do it,' I tell Michelle.

✱ ✱ ✱

INTRODUCTION

WHAT THE FUCK HAVE I DONE? Almost as soon as I've agreed, terror sets in. It's not the sitting down and writing part that's scary — it's the inescapable fact that I will have to think real hard about the past and then, even worse, focus on it, reflect on it and write about it. There will be a deadline and I will have to produce this quite big scary thing by that date.

But I can't go back now, and soon I'm opening every can of worms that ever existed from the past 34 years. Some cans are wormier than others, and because I promised myself I'd go into this with brutal honesty — because otherwise what's the point? — there's nowhere to hide. I cringe as I relive past humiliations, my face burning as I recall the little details of my past that make up the big picture. Why would anyone willingly put themselves through this? There is clearly something very wrong with me to have agreed to this.

I find it's actually quite annoying having to think about the bits of my life that weren't much fun. You know, the parts you think you've firmly locked away and never need to think about again? It turns out that when you write a book about yourself you can't pretend the hard stuff didn't happen. It also means I have to talk to the people I love about some of the things that have hurt me. And I start to feel really sorry for the poor person holding my hand through all of this. She has to sit through all my shit stories. And patiently wait for me to stop crying so I can finish my sentences.

It's not too bad at the start, because the due date is so far away that the whole thing feels mystical. Like a funny little fantasy that'll never come to fruition. But as the book takes shape and it becomes clear it's actually happening, I get overwhelmed. I start dreaming of disasters that could get me out of this mess. Maybe Covid will strike again and printing presses will close. Or the government might ban books. Especially ones about queer people. Unlikely, but a girl's got to hope. Maybe I could just run back to Australia, hide at Mum and Dad's house, and pretend I never agreed to this.

So, it feels quite ridiculous — or miraculous — that I now find myself working on the opening chapter of a book all about (gasp!) me. It's a book that's taken me on an emotional year-long journey. It's been fun to remember the funny situations I've been in, but it's also given me a newfound appreciation of the people in my life who've stuck with me even when I've been a complete basket case.

I knew it wouldn't be easy, but I didn't realise how exhausting it would be dragging out a shit-ton of secrets and demons from nooks and crannies I'd hoped never to see again. Often I found myself waking in the night, the book popping into my mind and me whispering 'This is a bad idea' as I lay awake in a cold sweat. But by the morning I'd have remembered another part of a story or reflected on something with a different perspective, and I couldn't wait to get into it again.

I love and hate this book in equal measure. I hate it because there's nowhere to hide, and that's confronting. But I love it because parts of my story feel important, to me anyway, and mostly because I hope my stories might help someone else.

INTRODUCTION

※ ※ ※

It's a Wednesday morning and I am getting my nails done. I'm at a salon just around the corner from my flat in Ponsonby. It's one of those fancy places — you know, not one of those cheap nail bars I'd usually go to. It's a fancy one where they do a beautiful job and it takes a bit longer. All the other ladies in there are wearing head-to-toe lululemon or full designer outfits that would make Carrie from *Sex and the City* want to be their friend. It's all a bit of a treat for me, because, you know, every turd needs rolling in glitter occasionally.

I do not dress for the occasion. I look every bit the scrubber from Queensland that I am, wearing my grotty denim shorts with an elasticated waistband, and a comfy old T-shirt. I'm sitting in the pedicure chair and I notice an older lady having her toes done a few seats down. She is beautifully put together; one of those women who just oozes rich. She's wearing an elegant, neutral-coloured linen dress and has an expensive handbag on her lap. This woman keeps glancing at me, and I feel judged. Maybe I should have brushed my hair. Or changed my T-shirt. I know she's looking at me but I avoid eye contact because I don't have the energy for anything hard today.

The lady doing my nails puts those hideous toe-separating sandal things on my feet and it's time to shuffle over for my manicure while the toe polish dries. As I'm doing this, awkwardly manoeuvring my body out of the pedicure chair and on to the cold tiled floor, the fancy woman who's been staring at me stands up and approaches. I feel nervous, like she might be about to tell me off.

'Are you Bree? Are you from the radio and TV?' she asks. I nod gingerly.

'I just have to tell you, I listen to your radio show, I watch *Celebrity Treasure Island* and I follow you on social media. And I really love what you do. So does my husband.'

Wow, this is unexpected — 60-year-olds are not in my usual demographic. I wonder if she's a fan of my fart jokes.

She continues: 'I want you to know, you've really helped me. You've helped me with a very hard situation. My daughter is gay. And I haven't handled it well, I've struggled with it, and I wasn't very nice to her about it. I found it very hard to accept. But seeing you be so open about who you are on your social media and on radio, and getting to know you . . . well, it's helped me understand my daughter more. And it's helped me see she's still my daughter, she's the exact same person, and I need to accept her for who she is. I just want to thank you for that because our relationship was very broken, but it's a lot better now.'

And this, folks, is why I ended up deciding to write this book. This is why I said yes. Not because this lovely lady then paid for my mani and pedi — although that was very kind — but because it reminded me why I do what I do. Why I make a dick of myself on radio, TV and social media. Why I talk about my partner Sophia, who happens to be a woman. And why I fart loudly in front of people and share it on Instagram. It reminded me that being open about who I am, and making people laugh

INTRODUCTION

in the process, can actually make a difference to someone's day. And that is the best feeling in the world.

When I was a young, awkward kid muddling through life, I always had a sense that I was alone. I felt like the only weird kid at school. There was something different about me. I didn't look right; I didn't fit in. In my teens, I wondered if there was something inherently wrong with me that made me the way I was. And in my twenties, I kept secrets so big that they bred shame like nothing else. If I'd known then that others were going through stuff too, I wouldn't have felt so alone. And isn't that what all of us are chasing? That feeling of not being alone?

So if someone can pick this book up and relate in some little way, that's a win for me. If it might help a kid, a young person, a parent, just someone (or more than one person, preferably, for the shit-ton of effort that's gone into it), then it's worth stepping out of my comfort zone and sucking up the discomfort.

If you're like me and can't possibly imagine reading a book from start to finish, don't worry. I won't judge you if this is as far as you get. But please, whatever you do, don't call this bloody thing a 'memoir'. It's a collection of silly little stories from my silly little life. I might regret sharing some of them — but that's my problem, not yours.

BREE

Oh, Brianna!

I call Mum from the car. 'Mum, listen, I've been pulled over by the cops for speeding. I've told them you've had an accident and that's why I was going too fast.'

'What on earth, Brianna?' says Mum, trying to figure this out.

'Mum, seriously, you have to help me. The cops are following me home and I've told them you've had a serious accident! Don't ruin this for me! I'll be in so much trouble.' I hang up and keep driving towards home, cracking up already at my comedic brilliance.

I turn into the driveway, pull up outside the door and run inside. I'm unsure of what I'll find, but I needn't have worried. Mum has really outdone herself. She's lying on the floor by the kitchen bench, groaning and moaning, crying for help. Two kitchen stools are lying on their sides, and she's even taken one sock off to prove the impact of her crash. Weird, but I appreciate the commitment.

I take one look at her and burst into laughter. She looks confused. Then she looks behind me to check for the police, and that's when she realises she's been had. There were no cops. No speeding.

'Oh, Brianna!'

* * *

I've been annoying Mum since 2 a.m. on 3 January 1989, when I broke her tailbone as I made my way out of her womb and into the world. Mum and Dad named me Brianna Stephanie Tomasel. Daughter of Stephen and Dianne, sister of Amber, who'd arrived just eighteen months ahead of me. My little brother Aden came along three years later.

To my family I'm still Brianna, but outside of Stanthorpe, Queensland, where my parents have lived their entire lives, I'm Bree. I was rebranded at thirteen by a softball coach who preferred the snappier version. I was delighted to be given my first nickname by someone I looked up to, so I ran with it.

My sister Amber was a quiet, adorable and easy-going child; the perfect firstborn. Sadly for Mum and Dad, I was the opposite to Amber. A screaming, yelling, in-your-face kind of kid from the word go. I was a 'look at meeeeee!' kinda gal. I was your classic attention-seeking middle child before Aden even came along.

'You just had more energy than most children,' Mum says, generously, when I ask what I was like when I was little.

What she means is that I drove her crazy a lot of the time. I think I drove everyone crazy, actually, because when I was little, Nonno and Nonna — my Italian grandparents — started calling me 'Little Terramoto'. *Terremoto* means earthquake in Italian. Dad gave me another nickname, too, which has stuck to this day: Pumpkin. After Punky Brewster, that ballsy little kid from that classic '80s TV show.

Even though I was high-energy and always on the hunt for attention, Mum says it wasn't all bad because I was funny, too. I hammed things up, I loved putting on little shows or making my own movies on the family video camera. Writer, producer and lead role all went to *moi*, of course! Boredom was my enemy — I couldn't handle having nothing to do. Even as a toddler, Mum says, I was the first to do things — whether it was jumping into the water from the bank, rolling down a hill or climbing to the top of a tree. She also says she'd thought I'd end up being a courtroom lawyer because I could argue till the cows came home.

Population 5000ish, Stanthorpe was — and still is — an ordinary little rural Aussie town, located on the New England Highway 217 kilometres south of Brisbane. There's not a lot there other than what you can see on the main road that passes through town — four pubs, a chemist, a supermarket, a post office, a doctors' surgery and a few other shops — but it was the perfect place to grow up. Stanthorpe finally got a McDonald's when I was about sixteen and opening day was the biggest event in the history of the town. That medium McChicken meal tasted like a unicorn sliding down a rainbow for this country kid.

I loved to roam; and luckily for me (and my parents, who were always keen to see the back of me), I had places to go because we lived on a sprawling apple orchard on the outskirts of town. I'd take off in the morning and could easily be gone for the whole day. Us kids had a dam to swim in, and we'd make huge mudslides down the sides of steep banks and into the water. We'd catch eels and yabbies from the creek, build forts and play epic games of hide and seek with the kids who lived on the farms around us. It was the perfect place for a girl like me who couldn't sit still. I look at photos of me from when I was small and I look like a little bush pig. Untamed hair, bare feet and usually covered in mud.

We lived in a typical Queenslander. Perched up on stilts and with the classic wraparound veranda, our house had a green corrugated-iron roof and burgundy trim. There must have only been two paint colours in those days because everyone else's houses were painted the same. Mum loved that house. She and Dad renovated it when I was about eleven, turning it from a shitty, cold and damp little farm cottage to a nice big family house with a bedroom for each of the kids. Mum was most proud of her shiny wooden floors, guarding them with her life and making sure we knew all about it if one of us left a mark. The floors matched the hideous timber kitchen that Mum and Dad bought secondhand because they'd run out of money for a new one.

Dad was obsessed with two things in life: the orchard and the weather. He couldn't talk about one without the other. If the weather was good, with just the right amount of sun and the right amount of rain, he was happy. If the weather was bad, he was not happy. And if a hailstorm hit, it was the end of the world. A hailstorm could wipe out an entire year's crops and earnings for our family, and Dad lived in fear of them. When dark clouds appeared in the sky they would match the dark clouds of Dad's mood. We all learned pretty young that if the weather was shit, you'd best stay out of Dad's way.

Dad's Italian, and Mum's an Aussie. Growing up, we were surrounded by both sides of the family. Mum's parents, Nan and Pa, were fifteen minutes down the road in one direction, and in the other direction were Nonno and Nonna, my dad's parents who'd migrated from Italy in the 1950s. Their brothers and sisters were all nearby, and thanks to the Catholic commitment to rampant breeding we had Italian cousins everywhere. If you'd asked me as a kid, I'd have thought it didn't get any better than what we had in Stanthorpe. There were 30 kids at our tiny country school, Pozieres primary. There were two classes with a teacher each, and we were all thrown in together; the older kids in one class and the younger ones in the other. In my grade, there were three boys and me. I would have loved a few female friends but it wasn't to be.

Mum was a hairdresser, but when us kids came along she gave it up to stay home and raise us. I've heard her say, 'If my kids are happy, I'm happy.' And that was pretty much her goal — if she could keep us three content and healthy, then she knew she'd done her job. She also used to say she had no bloody choice but to stay home and look after us because Dad was a workaholic. He'd get up before the sun rose, pull on his Blundstone work boots and head out on to the farm. He'd be gone all day, finally walking back in the door just in time for dinner. He did that seven days a week, 365 days of the year (with maybe a half-day off for Christmas and Easter — he is a Catholic, after all!). That meant it was Mum who drove us to our sports practices, Mum who was on the sidelines at games, Mum who turned up to the parent–teacher meetings, and Mum who cooked every bloody meal for us.

Mum is a trooper because she never ever complained. She loved being a mum. She was kind, generous, loving and, she admits now, probably spoiled us a bit because we didn't have to lift a finger. She did it all. Mum was determined to help us live our best lives. She took us anywhere we wanted to go and encouraged us to sign up for whatever activity we wanted, even if that meant letting me take saxophone lessons. I was a horrible musician. I had no talent whatsoever, and when I practised at home Mum had to ram bits of toilet paper in her ears.

Family holidays weren't really family holidays because Dad usually didn't go on them — he stayed home to work on the farm. Don't get me wrong: he loved us, and he was a wonderful dad. But he'd inherited the migrant 'work your arse off' mindset. He knew what his parents had sacrificed to give him the life he had and there was no way he was going to waste that by letting the orchard fail. Even though Mum and Dad left the farm about six years ago, they didn't opt for retirement — they just switched out the apple orchard for running cattle. And Dad hasn't changed; he's still obsessed with his land. He's had a hip replacement, a double knee replacement and a shoulder reconstruction, to name a few, yet he still works twelve-hour days. There's no stopping him. He says he's dedicated. Mum says he's mad.

As a kid, my sister's bedroom walls were covered with posters of the boys she was lusting over. Hotties like Jonathan Taylor Thomas (you know, Randy from *Home Improvement*) and Leonardo DiCaprio. I liked them too; they were cute enough. But at age ten, my heart belonged to one person and one person only. Her name was Anna Kournikova, the Russian tennis star, and she stole my heart the moment I saw her. I liked watching tennis — any sport is worth watching if you're a Tomasel — but when it involved Anna Kournikova it was a NOT TO BE MISSED event. Bigger than the Olympics, bigger than State of Origin and bigger than the FIFA World Cup. I didn't give a shit that Anna Kournikova was a fairly average player, I just thought she was the most magnificent woman in the world. I was obsessed with her and I didn't really know why. Of course, she was one of the biggest sex symbols in the world at that time so my crush was far from original, but still, to me, Anna Kournikova was everything.

Much to my annoyance, my family didn't have one of those flash VCRs that could record programmes off the TV, but Nan did. And because she was a saint of a woman who would do anything for her grandkids, she recorded every single match that Anna played for me. At the weekends, I'd get Mum to drop me over at her place. I'd plonk myself down on Nan's old brown couch and watch replays of Anna's matches on repeat, transfixed by this perfect specimen. Nan would deliver me a bowl of rockmelon doused in sugar (the only way to eat melon, according to Edna) and I was as happy as a pig in shit.

If my Anna Kournikova fixation wasn't a red flag for future lesbianism then I don't know what was, but back then I didn't think twice about whether it was weird to have a crush on a girl. I didn't even know it was a crush, and no one in my family seemed to raise an eyebrow at the hours I spent ogling a hot female tennis player. Besides, back then, I barely knew that homosexuality existed. I'd certainly never come across a gay person, either in real life or on TV, in books or at the movies. All I knew about 'the gays' was that Dad didn't seem to be a fan of them. 'Them' being poofters, fags and homos. If someone was taking too long to get up off the ground in a game of rugby, Dad would yell, 'Get up, ya poofter!' If a man on TV seemed a bit effeminate, according to Dad he must be a bit of a homo. And if there was any suggestion that a bloke might be in a relationship with another bloke, I got the distinct impression that in Dad's eyes that wasn't okay. Even at eight or nine years old, I knew that being one of these types wasn't something to aspire to. Poofters, fags and homos, I worked out, were not normal, not acceptable and certainly not the type of people my dad wanted anything to do with.

I love my dad. He is warm, hilarious, generous and loving. He is also a devout Catholic, which is to be expected for the son of Italian immigrants. Italians and Catholicism go hand in hand, much like Leonardo DiCaprio and girls under the age of 25 — you can't have one without the other. It's at the heart of their identity, it's who they are, and life without the Catholic Church (or in Leo's case, under-25-year-old supermodels) wouldn't make sense.

The Tomasels went to church every single weekend, their kids were sent off to Catholic boarding schools, and when Mum met Dad she had to convert to Catholicism to marry him. When we came along, Amber, Aden and I instantly became little Catholics, too. We were baptised at St Joseph's in Stanthorpe — the same church where Mum and Dad were married — and we traipsed along there each week to recite our prayers, sing our hymns and promise to devote ourselves to our Saviour Jesus Christ. We took part in nativity plays, and when we were about seven we had our First Communion. For months in advance we went to special lessons, and on the big day, when all the proud-as-punch parents and grandparents came to watch their little God-fearing angels drink the wine and eat the bread at their first Mass, all the good little girls looked sweet in their miniature wedding dresses made of white lace and tulle. Everyone apart from me, that is. I wouldn't be seen dead in a dress, and somehow got away with wearing purple silk trousers and a frilly white top.

I hated everything about church. I hated the musty smell, the sound of the priest droning on about nonsense I couldn't understand, the awful screech of the organ and the stern looks from the old biddies around us if we giggled or whispered. Mum was never that convinced about God either, but she went along with it because she knew how important it was to Dad. She remembers him telling her soon after they met that if he didn't go to church he would go to hell. Or, worse, purgatory — that terrifying limbo he was told about in great detail as a child to discourage sinful behaviour. And he really believed it.

By the time us kids hit our teens, we told Dad we'd had enough. We couldn't stand going to that bloody church any longer and we told him he couldn't force us. Mum got involved too, and told Dad that maybe it was time for us to be able to make our own choices. He was so angry he punched a hole in the wall at home. We were shocked — it was so out of character for him. But it showed just how much his religion meant to him. After a while, he gave up the fight. I think it had already dawned on poor old Dad that none of his children had inherited the devotion gene. Now it's just at Christmas and the odd Easter when we'll suck it up and go along because we know it makes him happy.

Eventually Mum gave up on church too, so now it's only Dad who still trots off to church every week in his Sunday best. He bloody loves it. He loves being Catholic because it connects him to his family, his history and his Italian heritage. I think he finds all the things I hated about it — the smells, the sounds, the rules, the rituals and routines — comforting. Catholicism is a part of him; I get it. But I find it hard to understand how smart people like my dad can put aside the Church's history of sexual abuse and teachings on homosexuality. Who knows, things might have changed now, but Dad was brought up to believe that homosexuality is a sin. And that in the eyes of the Lord, loving someone of the same sex is wrong. He was taught that sinners would not be rewarded with a good afterlife.

And until I came along, I expect he never thought he'd have to re-examine those views.

Woggy-style

'*Buon appetito!*' Nonno would say from his spot at the head of the table every Sunday afternoon, where our big, noisy family gathered for lunch that would stretch into dinner. Surrounded by the Aussie-Italian family he loved, Nonno was in his element and he held court, telling stories and making jokes in his thick Italian accent. No one's wine glass was ever empty and even the kids were allowed a splash. 'It's good for them!' he'd say with a laugh when a parent protested, pouring us a little glass of the cheap stuff that Nonna bought in bulk.

Wine wasn't as easy to come by then as it is now, but Nonna had found a place just outside Stanthorpe that sold big, 10-litre plastic containers of the stuff. God knows where that wine came from — it smelt more like vinegar than grapes — but it was good enough for Nonna, who would buy one of red and one of white.

And every few weeks Nonno would be sent off to collect them. She always said it was for her cooking, but we all knew Nonna put a decent amount of it away herself. Aden and I were given the very important job of decanting Nonna's wine into brown glass bottles with metal caps, which she stored in cardboard boxes in the garage under her house. We'd sit down there, on the cold concrete floor of the garage, using a funnel to pour the wine from the plastic container into the bottles. We carefully positioned a splash bowl underneath to catch what we spilt and Aden and I, aged about seven and ten, would sip away from that splash bowl while we worked. We were red-faced and giggling by the time we'd done the job. I'm sure Nonna knew we'd been dipping into her vino, but she didn't give a shit. She just wanted her wine bottled.

Nonna was one of a kind. Her eyes would light up when she saw me. She'd pinch my cheeks, say something in Italian which I barely understood, and plant a sloppy kiss on my forehead. I'm sure the cheek-pinching was an act of love, but damn did it hurt! Nonna was also the bluntest person in the family. I once turned up at her place with freshly dyed black hair. She took one look at me and said, 'Brianna, your hair is so dark, it looks like shit. You will never get a boyfriend looking like that.' She was right, I never did get a boyfriend — but I don't think we can blame that on the hair dye now, can we?

Nonna might have been direct, but that didn't mean she didn't adore her family. She did, and she loved to show it through food. Nonna's cooking is the stuff of legend in our family; we spent all week looking forward to her three-course Sunday feasts that she started preparing days in advance. There was homemade gnocchi and pasta, minestrone with piping-hot chicken broth. Porchetta and polpette, roast chicken and veal cotoletta. Crispy roast potatoes cooked with lemon and herbs, chicken simmered in passata made from her incredible tomatoes and bread to mop up the juices. Even her salads were special — homegrown leaves and herbs dripping with oil and vinegar. Nonna's humble kitchen was the engine room of the house and never in my life have I tasted food as good as what came out of there. I've spent years trying to make gnocchi like hers, chicken broth as delicious or potatoes as crispy, but no matter how hard I try it's never as good.

We would stuff our faces yet somehow always manage to fit in something sweet at the end, because Nonna also made what we all knew to be the World's Best Desserts. There was her special crostoli, crispy fried pastry dusted with icing sugar, which Nonna served with poached apricots or pears in sweet syrup. And her famous pastry turnovers with sweet, sticky apples picked from the tree outside her back door, or — my absolute favourite — Nonna's tiramisu, which I blame my love handles on to this day.

Mealtimes were taken seriously at Nonna and Nonno's house and were not to be rushed. Us kids would be sent off to play between courses while the adults stayed at the table, drinking wine and talking over each other in a wild mix of English and Italian. Mum would get increasingly pissed off the more Italian they spoke. She didn't understand a word and was paranoid they were talking about her. Maybe they were!

Nonna's cooking was magic, but the funny thing is that back then we all thought it was normal to eat this way. Half the kids in town were Italian and my school was crawling with Morellos, Arcidiaconos, Finocchiaros... us Aussie-Italians were everywhere. It wasn't till I left Stanthorpe for boarding school in Brisbane that it dawned on me not everyone had a family like mine, where sentences were begun in one language and finished in another. I also discovered that not everyone's grandparents lived in a house with Grecian columns out the front, gold-plated taps and door handles, faux marble benchtops, tacky chandeliers and carpet with a wild red-and-gold swirl. Nonna and Nonno's home could only be described as 'woggy-style' — a distinct kind of bogan-flash favoured by Italian and Greek immigrants. I think they loved it because it proved just how far they'd come.

* * *

Okay, who's up for a little history lesson? In the 1950s, Australia needed people — the workforce had been wiped out by World War II, so the Australian government launched a global campaign to encourage people to immigrate. 'Populate or perish' was the motto, according to Dad, who loves talking about his family history almost as much as the weather. Luckily for Australia, there was a shit-ton of people in post-war Europe who were so desperate to leave that they were prepared to make the long journey Down Under. My grandparents, Antonio (or Bruno as he was always known) and Adelina Tomasel, were some of those people. They lived in Treviso in the northern part of Italy. It's a beautiful place, often described as a mini-Venice because of the pretty canals that run through it, along with the historic palaces, medieval city walls and narrow cobbled streets. It's also famous for its prosecco. But back then, the area had been pretty much destroyed by the war, unemployment was high and most people were struggling to survive.

When they married, Adelina was 23 and Bruno 32. He'd spent seven years in the army, mainly in the artillery division fighting in Albania. Dad says Nonno never liked to talk about his time during the war, but Dad and his siblings managed to glean bits and pieces over the years. He was captured by the Americans once and by the Germans once, and in 1943 became a prisoner of war on the island of Sardinia. As the family legend goes, he was only there a few days before he managed to escape and make it back to Treviso.

Bruno's new wife Adelina was a bad-ass bitch, a fiercely ambitious woman with huge drive and motivation. She knew they would not get ahead in life by staying in Treviso — there were no jobs, no opportunities — and she didn't want to raise their future kids there. 'We have to get out of here,' she told her husband, who was determined to enjoy life again after the horror of war. With four brothers already living in Australia, Adelina made up her mind that this was where they needed to go. Bruno agreed — because, you know, happy wife, happy life — and in 1949, he and Adelina, who was several months pregnant by then, said goodbye to their families and everything they knew, and boarded a converted troop ship that had been repurposed for transporting thousands of fleeing Italians Down Under.

It was a trip from hell. The journey took almost four weeks. Men and women lived in separate quarters, sleeping in massive dormitories, with rows and rows of triple-tiered bunks to cram in as many humans as possible. The ship was old and filthy, and there was zero privacy. Passengers were fed canned food for every meal and people were getting sick everywhere you looked. The trip got even worse when the ship was hit by a cyclone off the coast of India. With all this made worse by morning sickness, Nonna hated every minute of it.

With everything they owned stuffed into one trunk and one suitcase, Bruno and Adelina finally disembarked at Sydney and took a train to Wallangarra in Queensland, where they were met by Adelina's brother Angelo Vedelago, who took them on to their new home of Stanthorpe. Nonna's four brothers had been in Australia for several years by then and were well set up. If there was one thing every Italian could do well, it was growing vegetables, so that's what most Italian migrants did once they arrived on Aussie soil. Angelo and his brothers started by growing veggies in the summer to sell at roadside stalls, and when winter came along they'd head to North Queensland to join worker gangs harvesting sugar cane. It was hard and dirty work. 'The sort of work the Australians didn't want to do,' Nonno always said.

By the time Bruno and Adelina arrived, Angelo had earned

enough money to buy a big property in Stanthorpe. He gave my grandparents work and a place to live, but made it clear there was no such thing as mate's rates or family passes. They would have to pay back the 70 pounds they owed him for their passage over. That was the equivalent of a year's wages back then.

Angelo was a shrewd businessman and had a gang of 40 workers who he'd also sponsored to migrate from in and around Treviso. Every single worker was desperate to go out on their own, so they worked like maniacs to pay back their debts and start saving money. It wasn't unusual for them to work twelve- or fifteen-hour days planting the orchard, tending the huge vegetable gardens, harvesting, and selling the produce at stalls. Dad always said that northern Italians were the most ambitious and there was no way they'd go all that way to sit around doing nothing.

But the culture shock for Nonno and Nonna must have been overwhelming. The little town of Stanthorpe — not much more than a dusty main road with a pub, a general store and a post office — was nothing like Treviso. There were no bakeries, delis or trattorias, and coffee came in powdered form only. They were terribly homesick, and it didn't help that they had not a word of English between them.

After about a year, Bruno was sick to death of working for his brother-in-law. With help from another of Adelina's brothers, he and Adelina finally bought their own little piece of land. They also started breeding like rabbits, and soon there were five little Tomasels — Renata, Dennis, Hugo, Stephen (my dad) and Ricky.

***

Dad might have been born in Aussie, but when he started school at six years old he didn't know a word of English. And he was petrified. Nonno dropped him off with his older siblings each morning, but by 10 a.m. he just had to get out of there. He couldn't understand a word of what the teacher was saying, and had no clue how to make friends when he didn't speak their language. Even opening his lunchbox was stressful because the other kids would tease him about his salami sandwiches. 'What's that shit he's eating?' they'd screech. Little Stephen became a master at escaping, somehow managing to sneak out the classroom door without the teacher noticing and running the three kilometres home. He'd turn up puffed and sad at the front door, where a furious Nonno would put him in the car and drive him straight back to school.

Nonno got crankier and crankier but nothing seemed to help Dad settle, other than time. It took a year before he started picking up English and making some friends. Nonna and Nonno finally decided it might help things along if they took some English lessons, too, though Italian was always the first and only language ever spoken in their home.

Back then, Thursday in Stanthorpe was known as 'Wog Day' by the locals, because that was the day when every Italian family went to town to do their shopping. Weirdly, no one in my family seemed to mind the word 'wog'. It might have started with racist intentions, but Dad can't remember a time when the word had any power at all. In fact, Dad says he always thought 'wog' was used affectionately by the born-and-bred Stanthorpe Aussies. And he was proud of being a wog. It was what made him and his family different.

Nonna and the other Italian mammas spent a lot of time complaining about the lack of decent ingredients to cook with. They couldn't get the things they were used to, like olive oil, Parmigiano cheese, ricotta, or anchovies in oil, so they had to be inventive. Every Italian family had their own pigs, which they used to make cured meats like salami, pancetta, prosciutto and mortadella. Nothing was wasted — the pig lard was used in place of olive oil. If Nonna wasn't in her kitchen, she would be in her veggie garden, bent over, weeding and sowing seeds and tending her vegetables. She grew everything herself that she needed to cook with: lemons, tomatoes, artichokes, fava beans (broad beans), zucchini, broccoli, spinach, peas, potatoes, and every herb you could imagine — basil, sage, parsley, marjoram, oregano, thyme. You name it, she grew it.

Food was Nonna's connection to her old life and home; it was her way of keeping her Italian heritage alive. When I think of her now, I imagine her holding a string of invisible spaghetti stretching from her kitchen in Stanthorpe all the way to Treviso. It was through food that Nonna eventually began to assimilate into the local community. She and Nonno would go to dances in the local hall. While Nonno swung the ladies around the dance floor and charmed them all, Nonna would talk — in her broken English — about food. She started to invite these ladies over for cooking lessons, and they loved it because up till then they'd never seen pasta, risotto, or the thin, flavoursome broths like the ones Nonna made. She taught most of her grandchildren how to cook, taking us into the kitchen with her and showing us how she worked her magic. We learned to make pasta on the bench, cracking eggs into mounds of flour and kneading and rolling till our wrists ached. She showed us how not to waste a thing, saving bones and old vegetables for soups and stocks, a pot of broth always simmering on the stove.

When Nonna got Parkinson's disease towards the end of her life, she couldn't cook anymore and I really saw the light go from her then. Without her garden and her stove, she didn't know who she was, or what her purpose was, anymore.

* * *

When Dad got a bit older, he realised not everyone liked immigrants like him and his family. At high school, he and the other Italian boys got picked on. They had racist abuse thrown at them every day in the playground. While the word 'wog' seemingly had no power, 'dago' was another thing altogether. Nonno had told his children never to tolerate that word, so Dad got into punch-ups every single day for the first six months he was there. He and his Italian mates formed a bit of a pack, and they never backed down when other kids were picking on them. By the end of the first year at school, the bullies gave up. It also helped that Dad was good at rugby. Eventually people started to forget he was a wog and instead he was accepted by the Aussie kids.

Dad later moved to a Catholic boarding school in Brisbane. Here, it wasn't the other kids he had to worry about — it was the nuns. The school was run by Irish Catholic Sisters of Mercy, but there was nothing merciful about these ladies. Dad says they were brutal. If he and his mates stepped out of line, they'd be lined up in front of the class and given eight whacks across the back of the legs with the wooden stick of a feather duster. It didn't take much to set the nuns off; Dad says it wasn't uncommon to have lash marks that would last for weeks. That sounds fucking miserable to me, but Dad says it was all part of growing up.

As Dad was so good at sport, he was going to become a physical education teacher when he left school. But Nonno said 'Why don't you work to save some money for a year first?' and got him a job with a builder. Dad was back home in Stanthorpe saving for college when he met my mum, Dianne. They were both eighteen, it was at a New Year's Eve dance and even though he'd gone with another girl, the minute he saw Dianne he knew she was the girl for him. Or something like that. They were never apart after that, and in 1981, when they were 23, they were married at the Tomasel family's beloved church, the gorgeous bride beaming alongside her tall, handsome, olive-skinned husband.

Dianne was certainly not the Italian that Nonna had in mind for her son, but he was in love and there was no arguing with that. Her conversion to Catholicism probably helped, too.

Terror

Life as a kid in Stanthorpe was good — until it wasn't. When I was about nine everything changed, both for me and my family. Something so awful and scary and unexpected that even now I still find it hard to think about, let alone talk about. But I know that this incident is what flicked my anxiety switch. Before that day, I was a happy-go-lucky kid. Not a care in the world, honestly. After it, I became a bundle of bloody nerves — and that's putting it lightly. I haven't been formally diagnosed with post-traumatic stress disorder, but I'm pretty sure that's what I've been dealing with ever since.

It was a Monday, the day before the Melbourne Cup. I should have been at school, but instead I was at home with a sore tummy. This wasn't unusual for me, as I'd been having stomach pains for weeks, maybe even months. The pain would creep on slowly, becoming so severe at times that I'd be bent over double, screaming in agony, and nothing seemed to help. The only pattern to the pain was that it usually came on after I'd eaten. Sometimes the pain would last a few minutes, whereas other times it would go on for hours. It was weird and worrying and I hated it because it was interfering with my life. By my life, I really mean my sport, which was pretty much what I lived for back then.

After a few weeks, or maybe a few months, Mum and Dad were getting worried. They took me to a bunch of doctors in Stanthorpe but no one could work out what was wrong. One doctor even suggested I was faking it to get out of school. Mum was like, 'Are you kidding? This kid loves school.' And she was right: the idea of faking an illness so I could bunk off school wouldn't have crossed my mind. I did love school. Eventually, Mum realised she wasn't going to get me the help I needed in our little country town, so she took me first to a doctor in Toowoomba, a couple of hours away, and then to Brisbane to see a specialist. After a whole bunch of scans and tests, it was discovered I had a severe ulcer that had taken over three-quarters of my stomach. No wonder it hurt when I ate. So much for faking it, eh?

Anyway, there I was, home from school and, for some reason, my brother Aden was there, too. Mum decided that instead of letting us sit around watching TV all day, we would go into town to visit Nan and do the banking on the way. Mum was in charge of the farm accounts, and once a week she'd go to the Stanthorpe branch of the National Australia Bank to deposit the week's takings. She also did a few ladies' haircuts at home some weeks, so she had money from that as well. The bag was pretty full that day.

Everything felt normal. The sun was shining and the cicadas were as noisy as ever as we climbed into the car to head into town. Aden and I waited in the back seat while Mum went into the bank, the radio left on to keep us occupied for the five minutes it would take to make the deposit and have a chat to the teller. 'Alright kids, all done, off we go,' she said, hopping back in the car and throwing her handbag onto the passenger seat.

We pulled up outside Nan's, and Aden jumped out first. He didn't even bother coming inside, instead running straight to the backyard to play on a tyre swing that hung from one of her huge eucalyptus trees. We loved those swings. I would have usually joined him, but instead I grabbed my schoolbag and headed into Nan's, where I sat down at the bright-green kitchen table she'd painted herself and pulled out my homework book. It was unlike me to be this diligent, but I'd had so much time off school with my sore tummy I was getting behind. 'Good girl, Brianna,' said Mum, sitting down opposite me. She and Nan chatted while Nan pottered about making the tea.

All of a sudden there was a knock at the door. Nan wasn't expecting anyone, but people often popped in unannounced in Stanthorpe; it was that sort of town. 'I wonder who that could be,' said Nan, heading through the kitchen to the front door. Nan was not a little-old-lady sort of grandmother. She was sturdy and strong. She had opinions and she wasn't afraid to express them. Pa had died a few years earlier and even though she was heartbroken, she knew she had to get on with life. 'I can't sit at home crying forever,' she used to say. Nan was like a second mum to us kids. She looked after us when Mum was busy and loved getting involved in our lives. She'd take us to the pool and get in with us. She was that sort of nan.

As soon as I heard Nan open the door, I knew something wasn't right. There was a commotion and I could hear men's voices. They weren't voices that belonged to anyone I knew.

'Where are your fucking keys?' someone yelled. My heart started to race, but before Mum and I could even react, two men appeared in the kitchen — one holding Nan in a sort of headlock and dragging her in alongside him. I knew she had to be scared but all I could think of was her hair. Nan had a perfect ashy brown perm that us kids were never allowed to touch. It was held in place with an entire bottle of hairspray. Now this guy had Nan's head in a vice-like grip and pulled tight against his chest.

'Hey!' yelled Mum, jumping out of her chair at the sight. But at that moment we both saw the knife. The man who had Nan was holding a knife to her throat. It wasn't a normal-looking kitchen knife — it was a big, rusty hunting knife with a wooden handle and a huge blade.

'We're going to die,' I told myself. 'We're going to die.'

It felt certain to me in that moment that these guys were here to kill us and there was nothing any of us could do about it. I looked out the window to where Aden was swinging higher and higher, pumping his legs and looking up into the tree above. 'Stay out there, Aden, stay out there,' I willed.

The men looked wild. Nothing like the type of people I was used to. They were scruffy and dirty and stank of filth and cigarettes. They were angry, but none of us could work out what they wanted with us.

Nan didn't fight or try to get out of the headlock. She looked calm, and Mum was the same. They must have been absolutely petrified, but they were desperately trying not to do anything to make things worse. And I'm sure they were trying to show me that we'd be okay. If they'd started losing it, god knows what I would have done.

'We'll give you whatever you want, just please don't hurt us,' Mum said, sitting back down in her chair across from me at the kitchen table.

It became clear they wanted the keys to our car parked outside in the driveway. It was a shitty old beaten-up Land Cruiser with 100,000 km on the clock, but they'd seen it from the road and that's what had lured them in. Mum handed the car keys across the table, but that didn't seem to be enough. They were now ranting about money and seemed to be getting angrier by the second. All I could think about was that knife still pressed up against Nan's throat.

After a bit, they told Nan to sit down. She chose the chair next to mine, sat down and strategically pressed her body against mine and wrapped her arms right over me to keep me safe, almost like she was turning herself into a human shield. The fear was overwhelming. My heart was pounding in my chest. I was trying to disappear, or at least be as quiet and small as possible so they didn't turn their attention to me, but giant tears were spilling down my cheeks and on to the table. I was angry with myself. I didn't want them to notice me and the sound of those huge tears hitting the table top was stressing me out.

The men were yelling now, screaming at us about keys and cash. 'We don't have any cash,' said Mum, over and over.

'You're fucking lying!'

Suddenly the atmosphere changed and one of the men came at me, grabbing me. He pushed Nan off, wrapped his disgusting arm around me and put me into a headlock. I froze, knowing there was no way out of it. Then I felt it — the cold sharp blade against my neck. I could feel the man's breath on the side of my face and the stench made me feel like I was going to be sick. I was going to die. I knew it. This was the end.

Mum jumped out of her seat again, but one of the guys screamed at her. She had to sit down and do what she was told. I looked up quickly, locking eyes with Mum for a split second. I don't know how she did it, but she still looked calm, and it was like she was channelling a message to me that it would be okay, that she would work something out. Slowly, Nan reached over to me and took hold of my hand. I gripped those comforting, dry, cold fingers like my life depended on it.

The other guy took off down the hallway and I could hear him ransacking the house. Drawers were flung open, all Nan's stuff was being thrown on the ground, her furniture hurled over, and doors were slamming. The guy holding on to me seemed to be getting more agitated, too; he was screaming about us being liars and demanding to know where we'd hidden all the cash. Mum was scared, and her calm facade was beginning to falter. She started begging the man to let me go. Again, she stood up.

'Sit *down* you dumb bitch!' he screamed. I felt the knife start to dig a little deeper into my skin. By now I was trembling. I felt like my body was shutting down and that any minute now I would melt into a puddle on the floor. Nan tightened her grip on my hand.

Again I looked out the window. Aden was still swinging, still oblivious to the danger inside. 'Stay there, Aden, stay there,' I said over and over inside my head.

Suddenly the man holding me spotted Mum's handbag on the floor at her feet. 'There's nothing in there,' she told him. 'Empty it,' he ordered. She tipped the contents on to the table. Keys, half-used lipsticks, a random sock . . . just the usual weird stuff you'd find in Mum's handbag. Plus, a wallet with no cash inside. Then he saw Mum's banking bag — a calico drawstring bag with the National Australia Bank logo on the front, like the one every Aussie farming family had. Thirty minutes ago it had held a few grand in cash. Now it was empty.

The man's eyes widened like he'd hit the jackpot, but when he found there was nothing inside he was enraged. 'You're fucking lying to me!' he screamed when Mum tried to explain there was no cash because she'd just done the banking that morning.

'She's not lying!' I wanted to scream, but nothing came out.

'You're fucking lying to me, you're *lying*. I'm taking your daughter, I'm taking her with us.'

He pulled me off my seat and on to my feet — the knife still at my throat — and dragged me towards the door. I didn't know whether to fight him or let myself get kidnapped. If I refused to walk, I knew he would kill me.

'NOOOOOOO!' I *was* screaming now. 'Mum, *help!* Don't let them take me!'

That was it — Mum was up out of her seat. Her voice was still calm, but I could see she had gone to another place. She was *not* letting this happen. She pushed past us and stood in front, stopping the man from taking me any further. 'I'll come with you,' she told the man. 'Take me, not her — I'll come with you, but you're not taking my daughter.'

It was no use. The prick who had me had switched to another level of crazy and his grip on me tightened. 'Fuck you, I'm taking the girl, fuck you!' he yelled.

Then the other guy appeared from down the hall. He seemed to have calmed down a bit and when he saw that his fucked-up mate was trying to kidnap me, he intervened. 'We're not taking the girl. Let's leave, let's get out of here — we've got what we need.'

It was over. They were gone. From that point on, my memory of the day blanks out. I know we had to go next door to get help, because those scumbags had ripped the phone from the wall. Me, Mum and Nan held hands and walked out to get

Aden, then went over to the neighbour's together, shaking like leaves and crying. Dad arrived, and the police turned up. No one could believe this had happened in our safe and sleepy little Stanthorpe. Nothing like this had happened before, and it probably hasn't happened since.

For me, nothing was ever the same again. The chilled-out happy kid had left the building and in her place was a terrified little girl who didn't feel safe again for a very long time.

* * *

A few days after it happened, the police found our Land Cruiser parked in the driveway where one of the guys lived. Those knob-jockey crims were clearly not the sharpest tools in the shed. It turned out they were from a place called Warwick, which is the next town over from Stanthorpe towards Toowoomba. They'd held up a service station the day before targeting us, so the police already knew who they were from the CCTV. We were told they were druggos looking for money and there was nothing personal in them choosing us. We were just in the wrong place at the wrong time — but try getting a nine-year-old girl who's been held at knifepoint to believe that. I was convinced those guys were out to get us and it was only a matter of time before they'd be back.

I'd never even watched a scary movie or thought about bad guys before, but now I had experienced true terror and it left its mark on me. Plagued by vivid, terrifying memories and flashbacks, I was now a kid whose mum had to sleep in her bed each night. Every single night for the next year, Mum would hop into bed with me and wrap her body around mine so I felt safe enough to let myself fall asleep. She would stroke my hair, promise me everything was okay, and she wouldn't fall asleep herself until she knew I had.

Most nights, I'd wake up several times with a racing heart, terrified that they were coming back to get us — and Mum was always there, right next to me in my bed, ready to calm me back down and reassure me I was safe.

But I couldn't get those guys' faces out of my head and I felt scared all the time. I was scared of the dark, scared of men I didn't know, scared of scruffy-looking people. Scared of pretty much everything. I didn't trust anyone outside the family anymore and hated being away from Mum. If I saw a man in dark clothes, I'd freak out. Any noise outside the window at night would leave me trembling. When we got our car back from the police, I opened the back door to climb in, but then I smelt them, those filthy stinking men. I could smell the sweat and the cigarettes and the foul breath. I screamed and cried and told my parents I would never get in that car ever again. Mum, of course, being the amazing mum that she is, took the car and got it professionally cleaned so it didn't smell anymore.

Nan's biggest fear after the horror was that I would be too scared to ever visit her again. But I did go back, perhaps because I knew that if Nan was brave enough to remain at home then I could be brave, too. Or maybe it was those Anna Kournikova replays.

UNAPOLOGETICALLY ME

* * *

A few weeks after the home invasion I had my first panic attack. Back then I didn't know what a panic attack was, of course, but looking back, that's what it was. It would be the first of many. It was a hot, sunny day at home, so I did what I often did and headed to the freezer for an ice block. Now, we weren't a rich family whose fridge in the kitchen had a freezer under it. Our freezer was a big old thing downstairs in the laundry, which was filled with piles of clothes, cobwebs and god knows what else. I didn't like going down there at the best of times, but I told myself to be brave, ducked down the stairs, grabbed a Fairy Floss Zooper Dooper (IYKYK, the GOAT of ice blocks) and ripped open the wrapper with my teeth. But then I noticed a little red spot on my hand. A tiny mosquito bite.

Absolutely nothing to worry about, right? Wrong. Seriously wrong, because as soon as I saw that little mark on my hand, I was tipped into a state of complete panic. My heart started racing out of my chest and the walls felt like they were spinning around me. 'MUM!' I managed to scream, collapsing to the ground sobbing and gasping for air. I didn't have a clue what was happening to me, but I knew I was about to die. Mum came running from the other end of the house. 'What's happened?' She looked terrified.

'I've been bitten by a poisonous spider. I'm going to die,' I managed to tell her through my tears and gasps.

For the record, I had *not* been bitten by a poisonous spider.

TERROR

It was a tiny mozzie bite. But something in my brain had turned against me, telling me that the little mark on my hand was fatal. And I believed it to be true.

Mum took a look at the tiny red mark on my hand and could see it wasn't anything to worry about, but that did nothing to calm me down. I was hyperventilating, sobbing and panicking. I'd lost the plot. Mum scooped me onto her lap and held me. She had no idea what was going on, but she held me and rocked me as I screamed, panicked and struggled to breathe, telling me over and over, 'It's okay, it's okay.' Afterwards I climbed into bed and stared at the wall for hours, wondering if I would ever feel normal again. I wanted to go back to being the girl I had been just a few weeks ago. I missed the lightness of who I used to be. Now I just felt scared *all* the time.

As part of the court case against the two men who did this to us, I had to go to a child psychologist in Brisbane so they could assess whether I'd suffered lasting effects. At one point, they asked me to draw a picture. 'Draw anything you like,' said the court-appointed psychologist, after an hour of talking about what I'd been through. I reached for a pencil and drew a detailed picture of people being stabbed and killed.

Talking about your problems — let alone having therapy for them — wasn't the sort of thing people did in rural Queensland back in those days, but Mum could see I needed help. She found a counsellor in town and convinced me to go. I wasn't keen, but I went for a few weeks or so. Weirdly, I don't remember anything about those sessions — I couldn't even tell you if the therapist was a man or a woman. All I know is that one day Mum picked me up afterwards and I was really angry. I hopped in the Land Cruiser, looked over at her and told her I was never going to the counsellor again.

'You know what, Mum? I'm sick of talking about it. I don't want to talk about it ever again.'

So that was that. It was the end of the counselling and it was the day I decided it was time to get over it. I was sick of feeling scared, sick of thinking about the home invasion, and I just wanted to be me again. I never, ever wanted to talk about what happened again, especially not with a stranger. I decided it was time to move on.

That was a nice idea, I guess, but the reality is I don't think I ever did get over what happened to me and Mum and Nan that day. Something in my heart or mind or deep inside me had changed. I wasn't carefree anymore. I was worried all the time, scared all the time. I was always ready to run or hide. I hated the dark. I didn't like loud noises, but I also didn't like silence.

Although I got really sick of feeling scared, nothing much helped other than time. Eventually, those tangible memories of the incident faded into the background and I was left with what I'd describe as a lingering sense of unease with the world. I was anxious a lot of the time, and there was a heaviness to the anxiety I carried around. I became quite negative about life; things that had never bothered me before really began to worry me. I would come up with a hypothetical thought about something bad that might happen, and I couldn't control it. Before long it would blow up into the hugest, most catastrophic thought, and would keep me awake at night.

This pattern of fatalist thinking has continued throughout my life, and while I didn't realise it back then, I know now that what happened that day changed me. I had discovered that bad things can and do happen. Those panic attacks struck me frequently, and still do. The anxious feelings build and build inside me until my brain tricks my body into falling apart. I feel like I'm having a heart attack — my chest tightens, my breathing becomes irregular and panicked, and even my limbs feel like they're not working. I can see why people take themselves to hospital when they first experience a panic attack, because in those terrifying moments you really believe you're dying.

Now I'm older I've recognised that the trauma of that home invasion has never really gone away. I always lock the front door behind me when I'm at home. I don't like being alone at night. And if I'm out in the evening, I walk to my car with my key between my fingers, ready for anyone who might be waiting to attack me. I know lots of women do this — but the difference for me is that I genuinely believe it's going to happen.

I know this because the worst *did* happen.

Tomboy Tomasel

The only thing keeping me from going completely nuts after the home invasion was sport. The only time I was truly able to put what had happened out of my mind was when I was running around playing soccer or softball, competing in athletics or even just kicking a ball around outside at home. I put my hand up for every sport, every team and every tournament. If there was a chance to play, I would grab it because I knew that when I was playing, I was happy.

Outside of sport, I was starting to feel different to other kids. I don't know if it was because of what I'd been through at Nan's, but I felt like I didn't fit in. I had a creeping suspicion that I wasn't 'normal' in the way other girls seemed to be. It didn't help that I really didn't like what I saw in the mirror. As far as I was concerned, I was as ugly as a bag of old spuds. I was awkward. I looked weird. I was too tall, too boyish. While other girls were trying to be fashionable, I didn't have a clue how to dress. My default outfit was a pair of crappy old shorts and a T-shirt, because that's what was comfortable. The older I got, the more socially awkward I became. School photo day was a nightmare. Everyone else dressed up and looked great, but I didn't know how to smile, hold my arms or where to look. Often it felt like there was a little voice inside my head making me doubt myself.

But when I played sport, that voice vanished and I was able to feel totally like myself. I knew I belonged and, even better, I could excel. Unlike friendships and social situations, the rules in sport were clear. If you played well, you got praised and people liked you. If you worked hard, you improved. I felt accepted in this world, so it made sense that I began to choose to spend every waking moment outside of school playing sport. Athletics, cross-country, tennis, swimming, softball, soccer, cricket, basketball, netball... you name it, I put my hand up for it. And the more competitive the situation, the more I loved it. I was pretty good, too, and it wasn't long before I was representing the district at state-level tournaments. At age ten I had won a few state championships for high jump and long jump. I went to the Pacific School Games and competed against kids from all around Australia. And as the bookcase in our lounge room started filling up with the trophies I picked up along the way, my obsession with sport kept getting stronger. If you'd asked me back then what I wanted to be when I got older, the answer would've been a professional athlete. There was nothing else that made me as happy.

Athletics was where I first started to shine but, over time, it was softball and soccer that became my main events. By my teens, I was playing at a pretty high level. My schedule was intense, with trainings and games every day of the week. Sport gave me a sense of purpose in a town where there really wasn't much else going on.

Being good at sport didn't earn me many friends, though. I stood out like a sore thumb because I was often leaving school early for training or to travel to national competitions. It set me apart, and the other kids didn't like that. They thought I believed I was better than them. Also, from a really young age I was playing in boys' teams because they didn't have a girls' soccer team.

'Look out for the big, mean, ugly girl,' yelled a boy in another team during a tournament. He was talking about me. I knew this because I was the only girl on the field during a match against another Queensland side.

Amazingly, the boys in my team didn't have a problem with me; it was the boys in the other team who seemed really pissed off about playing against a girl. Maybe they were scared I was going to be better than them, because we all know boys don't like being shown up by girls.

'Look at that big, mean, ugly girl,' the kid yelled again. Mum, sitting on the sidelines, was listening and her blood was boiling. She stood up and marched right up to that little shit, looked him straight in the eye and said, 'Excuse me, that's my daughter you're talking about. She might be big and she might be mean, but she's not ugly.'

Classic Mumma Di, always looking out for me.

It wasn't just the kids who were miffed by my presence on the boys' team; some of the parents didn't like it much either. Once, there was a dad on the sidelines who'd been getting increasingly frustrated because I was defending against his son, shutting down every move he attempted with the ball and making it impossible for him to score. 'Come on, son — she's just a girl!' he yelled from the sidelines. That egged me on even more. I was thinking, 'You just bloody watch me.' That kid didn't even come close to scoring a goal that day.

My reputation took a further dive after I accidentally broke a boy's collarbone during a game. This little shit had been giving me grief all game and he was desperate to shut me down whenever I got the ball. Finally, I saw a breakaway ball and thought, 'That's mine.' I sprinted across the field diagonally and went to slide in with my foot to pass it to a teammate. But, out of nowhere, this boy tried to get there at the same time and we collided. He went down with a broken collarbone. I muttered apologies as he was taken off the field, screaming, but secretly I thought that this little douche — who'd been talking shit at me all game — deserved to feel the wrath of Tomboy Tomasel.

As I've mentioned before, my family was as obsessed with sport as I was. If there was sport on the telly, we'd be there, curtains pulled, the five of us squished on the lounge ready to yell and cheer like the bat-shit Queenslanders we were. We would have watched competitive goat-herding if it had been on — it didn't matter what the sport was, it was all about the competition. Me,

Mum, Dad, Amber and Aden are all quite different people in our own ways, but the love of sport is something we have in common and it's bonded us.

There was another reason us kids loved watching sport with Mum and Dad, too. It was the only time we ever heard them swear. And I love that, it's pure passion and emotion — which is what sport's all about, isn't it? State of Origin brought out the bogan in all of us. And perhaps I'm being dramatic here when I say we would die for the Queensland Maroons, but it's not far off the truth. They are the greatest team to walk the earth. Cheering them on together as a family was one of the best feelings — and still is.

Even Nonno got into it. When it came to the NRL he had no idea about the rules, but he watched every game, screaming at the players in his hilariously broken English. He never sounded more Australian than when cheering on the Brisbane Broncos: 'Get in there, ya bloody bastards!'

The Olympics was also a massive deal in our house, so when Sydney hosted the games in 2000 it was bloody exciting — we'd waited years for this. We couldn't afford tickets for any of the events, so instead we planned a holiday around it, renting an apartment in Caloundra on the Sunshine Coast for two weeks with the sole purpose of watching every single minute of the Olympics. Even Dad dragged himself off the farm for a few days to join us. In between events, us kids would jump in the pool or run over the sand dunes to the beach for a swim, before hooning back to the lounge for the next event.

The biggest moment of Sydney 2000 is etched in my memory — it was the 400 metres race and Cathy Freeman, an Indigenous Australian, was competing. Athletics had never been Australia's thing, you know, but we all had a sense that something big was going to happen. The lights were turned off, the curtains pulled, and Mum, Dad, Amber, Aden and I sat nervously on the edge of the lounge. None of us said a word — we were all too nervous — but we gasped when Cathy appeared on the screen. She was wearing an incredible green and grey full bodysuit. The commentators were astonished, no one had worn anything like it before, but suddenly BANG! the starting gun went off and Cathy was just *flying*. We were all on our feet, screaming at the telly: 'Go Cathy, go! Do it for your country!'

She blitzed it, she won gold, and we were beside ourselves. We knew it was special. And at eleven years of age, I remember having the distinct feeling that anything was possible. If Cathy Freeman could make it to the top, so could I.

* * *

By the time I hit my teens, my downtime was filled entirely with sports. A typical weekend looked like this: I would get up at 4.30 a.m. on a Saturday and Mum would drive me to Toowoomba. I'd play two games of softball in Toowoomba and then I would stay the night with a friend, whose parents would drive us to Brisbane for more softball the next day. Mum would make the three-hour drive from home and meet me there, sitting on the sidelines for the whole six-hour training before driving me three hours home again. On the way I would change out of my softball gear into my soccer kit, arriving back in Stanthorpe just in time for a game of club soccer.

I don't know how I did it. I never moaned about the intensity of this life. And nor did Mum, even though she was spending eight hours in the car each weekend ferrying me around. Mum and I chatted so much on those car rides, and I'm sure it's one of the reasons why we're so close. I was aware at the time how lucky I was to have a mum who was prepared to do so much for me, and I still am.

Even though I was only fourteen, I had made the Under 16 Queensland softball squad. We would train together for a few months, with a smaller team selected at the end to represent Queensland at the Nationals. It was a BIG DEAL just to make the squad and I was totally determined to make it into the team. And I did — I made the team. Being named in that team was one of the best days of my life. I'd worked so bloody hard for it and I couldn't wait to compete at such a high level.

But I was determinedly ignoring a niggling pain in my lower back. I knew something wasn't right, but nothing was going to stop me training so I didn't mention it to anyone. I just kept on going, telling myself it was just a pulled muscle and it would come right. Every time I swung the softball bat, something in my back would go 'ping'. 'Ouch,' I'd think. But it wasn't bad enough to make me stop. I'd trained for months and months, so there was no way I was going to let a sore back get in the way of my dreams.

However, everything came to a crashing halt during one of the Sunday training sessions. Our team was playing a practice match against a boys' team. It was a close game, yet we were determined to win so every single one of us girls was playing as hard as we could. Someone hit a ball into the outfield, and as I was on third base I started to sprint. As I slid into home plate, I collided with a boy from the other team and he landed on top of me, crushing me as we hit the ground.

An incredible pain shot up my back and down my legs. It was agony like I'd never felt before and I screamed. I knew something very, very bad had happened because a numbness was spreading down my legs. They felt disconnected, as though they were no longer my own limbs. I was terrified, bawling my eyes out as I lay in the spot I'd landed and people came running from all directions. 'Don't move her!' yelled the coach. 'Call an ambulance!' someone else shouted. Mum ran onto the diamond and she was there kneeling on the ground next to me, trying to keep me calm but obviously freaking out as much as I was on the inside.

While Mum was worrying that I might never walk again, all *I* could think about was the Queensland team and the Nationals I was meant to be competing at. I knew it was all over for me. And I was completely and utterly devastated.

The ambulance crew arrived, and they put a neck brace on me and lifted me onto a spinal board to carry me to the ambulance. Someone had put a big block of ice down the back of my knickerbockers, but it didn't do shit to help the pain. It was intense. The drive to the hospital wasn't long, but I remember focusing on every turn, just praying the pain would be over with soon.

In the emergency department I was looked after by a total douchebag of a doctor. The first thing he did was make a joke about the block of melting ice that someone had shoved down my pants when I was screaming in agony on the field.

'What's this, have you wet your pants?' he said, with a smirk.

HA HA. Very funny, weirdo.

He did a few checks and sent me for an X-ray. When nothing obvious showed up, he sat down at my bedside and asked 'Are you sure it's not just period pain?' Did I mention that he was a douchebag?

After a few hours, Dr Douche told Mum there was nothing wrong with me and to take me home. I'd regained the feeling in my legs, but I could barely put weight on them because the pain in my lower back was extreme. Mum knew there was something more serious going on.

I felt like screaming. But instead I lay there in a miserable state while Mum quietly made a plan. As she does in any crisis, she took charge and figured out what to do next. She told the doctor: 'I know my daughter. There is something very wrong here, we're going to get a second opinion.'

She managed to get hold of a sports doctor and made an appointment for the next morning. He sent me straight for an MRI scan. 'You have suffered a very severe injury,' he told us in his consulting room afterwards. The scan showed that I'd fractured two vertebrae in my lower spine. I'd also suffered something called a 'spondy', short for spondylolisthesis, which is when a vertebra slips out of place and ends up resting on the bone below it. The doctor told me it was common in young athletes, but that mine was so severe I'd be unlikely to ever play sport at a high level again. He warned that contact sports would present a really high risk of even more severe injury.

Fuck. It wasn't just the Nationals I was missing out on — life as I knew it was over. Sport *was* my life. I was miserable at Stanthorpe State High but sport was my escape. I couldn't imagine life without it.

I cried for the whole two-and-a-half-hour drive home and so did Mum, tears streaming down her face as her hands gripped the wheel. It was hot as hell and our shitty old Land Cruiser's aircon didn't work, so we had the windows down and let the wind blast our faces. It was one of the first and only times I heard Mum use the F-word. 'You know what, Brianna? It's just fucking bullshit.' After that we didn't talk, just cried.

Secretly, I decided on that drive home that I would prove the doctors wrong. I *would* play sport again and I would still make it all the way to the top. I was determined not to let this shitty back injury ruin everything.

I threw myself into physiotherapy like a maniac, working hard to rebuild the muscles around my spine so that my core muscles and everything around were strong enough to give my damaged spine the support it needed. Mum took me to Toowoomba twice a week after school for intensive rehab sessions, and every day I worked hard at the exercises I was given. But being unable to play sport was torture. I'd gone from being the busiest teenager in the world to someone with absolutely nothing to do. I didn't have friends to hang out with or any other hobbies to turn my attention to. Unsurprisingly, I sank into a real low state, spending most of my time locked in my room listening to the saddest song in my CD collection, 'Breakaway' by Kelly Clarkson. I didn't socialise with anyone, I didn't even go and watch my old teams play. I couldn't face the world.

* * *

I was supposed to abstain from exercise for a year, but after nine months I thought, 'Fuck this.' I was going crazy, and I knew the only way I would feel better would be to start playing again. I rejoined the softball team. Mum was worried and so was the coach — they knew it wasn't entirely sensible. But there was no telling me. I was doing it, no matter what. The minute I picked up the softball bat or tried to throw a ball, though, I knew I wasn't the same athlete. My body wasn't as strong. I moved more gingerly and felt much more mentally timid. I hated it, and I felt so mad at myself. But I refused to give up; I just kept on pushing, and by the following year I reckoned I had a chance of making it back into the squad. 'Imagine if I could make it to the Nationals after all,' I thought.

I managed to get back into the Toowoomba team, which would compete in the tournament where the Queensland squad would be selected — just like the year before. Even though I knew I hadn't played anywhere near as well as I had before the accident, I was still holding out hope that my name might be on the list of girls read out on the last day.

At the end of the tournament, the coach, Bill Shorten, stood up and started reeling off girls' names. Twenty names in total, and Brianna Tomasel only featured at the very end — in the list of back-up players, the ones who hadn't made the squad but could get called up if someone dropped out. I'd failed, and I was absolutely heartbroken. I managed to hold it together until Mum got me in the car and then I fell apart. I don't think I've ever felt so devastated. I felt mortified to be excluded from a squad I'd made a year earlier. It was embarrassing.

Mum phoned Bill to ask him why I hadn't been picked.

'Bree is too much of a risk,' he said. 'We know about the severity of the injury and we can't risk losing her again like last year.'

I'd never liked him much — he wore his pants too high and was a bit of a loser. Now I absolutely hated him. But I sucked it up and trained with the squad as a back-up player, knowing full well that the chances of getting to the Nationals were pretty much zero.

In the end, I did go to the Nationals but not with my Queensland team. Instead I was picked up by the Tasmanian team, who needed extra players. There was a system where a state or territory that wasn't as well resourced could have access to good players from other states to help them be a bit more competitive. So there I was, playing at the Nationals against girls I'd trained alongside for the past few months. Tasmania wasn't strong, we had no hope of winning — but when I came face to face with my old team I gave it a red-hot crack.

It was 3–nil to them. When it was my turn to bat, we had two runners on base. I looked around at the faces of my old teammates, then over at their coach, Bill fucken' Shorten. The ball came flying towards me and I smashed it as hard as I've ever smashed a ball in my life. And it flew, it was absolutely *flying* as I dropped my bat and took off. Two runners ran in, and as I rounded second base there was no way I was stopping. I dived into third base, looked up — and locked eyes with Bill. I like to think that in that moment he realised what a terrible mistake he'd made. Probably not, though.

The game was tied at 3–3 and the Tasmanian supporters were going wild. I was thinking, 'Yeah, eat it up, Bill Shorten, you beady-eyed fuck.' It didn't last, though. They ended up coming back and beating us 5–3.

After that I continued playing softball and soccer, but I wasn't the same. I was good, but I wasn't great; and even though I made some decent teams in the following years, the excitement faded a bit. Reality had hit that I probably wasn't going to make it all the way to the top. My dreams of being a professional athlete had been stopped in their tracks by that bloody back injury.

Riding the crimson wave

You know how some girls are just desperate for their boobs to grow in? I was *not* one of those. I hated my changing body, so much so that when I was twelve I would wear two singlets to try to cover up the growing mounds that had suddenly appeared on my chest. I felt mortified by their appearance. 'How could this be happening?' I'd think, standing side-on in front of the mirror and feeling nothing but shame and horror at my new curves.

It was obvious that my body was changing but I did NOT WANT TO TALK ABOUT IT. Mum tried to have the period talk with me. 'GO AWAY,' I shouted in a hormonal rage. We were not a prudish household, but puberty was a topic I could not handle. I'd always been awkward, but boobs and pubes made things so much worse. I felt disgusted by myself. Everything felt so embarrassing and so shameful. And even though I knew that every girl would get their period one day, I hoped like hell I might be the exception to the rule.

Sadly I wasn't, and my little red friend arrived for the first time at the start of Grade 8, in my first year of high school. Aunt Flow didn't choose any old day to turn up, of course — she made her grand appearance the night before our school swimming carnival. I was good at swimming; I usually won a few medals, at least. This was terrible timing.

Obviously I couldn't tell Mum I was riding the crimson wave because that would have been too embarrassing, so I shoved a wad of toilet paper down my undies and headed off to school with a bag full of swim gear I had no intention of using. I felt like I was the only thirteen-year-old girl who had ever got her period and when I walked into school that day I was convinced everyone would know what was happening down below. Maybe if I'd had a best friend, I could have confided in her; but I didn't. If I'm honest, I didn't even have a close friend. I was friendly with some of the girls in my sports teams but that was about it. At primary school I'd played with the boys at lunch, but here at Stanthorpe State High things were different. Boys and girls didn't mix, so I was that misfit who would walk around at lunchtime pretending to be chill with being on my own, when on the inside I felt completely lonely and lost. I looked at the girls sitting in their groups and felt mystified about how they made it all look so simple. I wasn't shy so much as awkward. I didn't know what I was doing wrong.

As the swim races began, I went to my teacher and told her I felt sick. I spent the rest of the day in the stands. 'Why aren't you swimming?' other kids would ask when my races were called. 'I don't feel well,' I lied. I was a sad-sack sitting there feeling sorry for myself, the sodden toilet paper in my knickers reminding me what a freak I was.

When I got home, I flopped down on the lounge in a heap. Mum knew something was wrong and begged me to tell her what was going on. Finally, I muttered, 'I got my period.'

'Oh, Brianna!' She said all the nice things that mums say when girls get their periods, things that are actually a bit creepy — like, 'It's exciting, you're becoming a woman.' Then she bloody well offered to demonstrate how to use a pad, which was the final straw for teenage me. I locked myself in my room until the next morning.

This changing body sucked. I did not want to stop being a kid and I did not want to look like a woman. And to be honest, I had absolutely no idea how the rules of womanhood worked. I'd already been mocked at primary school for having hairy legs. Apparently I was the last person on earth to shave my legs. Where was the guidebook for this stuff? How was I supposed to know you're meant to start shaving your legs at eleven? The hairy-legs situation came to a head when I was selected for a softball trip away. I was going to be with a group of older kids and I knew I couldn't get on that bus with my legs looking like a yeti's. Obviously I couldn't talk about it with Mum, way too embarrassing, so I locked myself in the bathroom and grabbed one of Dad's plastic Bic razors. I dragged that thing up and down my dry legs, cutting them to shreds and bleeding all over the bathroom floor.

It's hard growing up. You look funny, you smell funny, your body is changing and you don't have a clue who you are and how you're meant to be. I don't miss that feeling.

✳ ✳ ✳

I might be a fully functional queer person now, but back when I was thirteen I was of the belief that romantic relationships came in one package: boy and girl. Man and woman. Husband and wife. If little Bree had looked into the future, which she tried not to do too often, she would have hoped to see the suburban set-up she was used to: Bree with a nice-enough husband, a couple of kids, a typically hetero sort of dog like a golden retriever, and a car in the driveway. But unsurprisingly, I was not someone who boys showed any interest in. Other girls were getting notes in their bags from boys inviting them for a pash after school. But not me. All I got was a shove in the hallway now and then.

One of my first crushes was a boy named Dylan. I was too shy to talk to him at school, but miraculously I managed to start a conversation with him on MSN Messenger, which was big at the time. He was good at sport, like me, so we chatted about that for a few days before I plucked up the courage to tell him I liked him. To my absolute delight and astonishment, he told me he felt the same way.

'Let's meet up after school tomorrow,' he said, suggesting the nearby cafe where all the cool kids gathered.

This. Was. Huge.

The next day I made my way to the allocated meeting place. I'd even got up early that morning to straighten my hair with the iron for the occasion. When I say iron, I don't mean an actual, proper hair-straightening iron. I mean Mum's iron, the one she ironed our clothes with. Let's be honest, though, you can roll a turd in glitter but it's still a turd, and I looked as rough as usual for my hot date with Dylan.

As I headed towards the cafe, I noticed a big group of the cool kids standing outside. Dylan was there, but he was surrounded by his mates and they were all pointing and laughing at me.

'You actually thought Dylan liked you?!' one of boys said as the laughing got louder.

The whole thing was a set-up. Of course Dylan didn't like me. I felt so stupid and it further confirmed my growing belief that I was likely to be a virgin for life.

* * *

Convinced I was unlovable, I nearly died of shock when I finally had my first kiss in Grade 9. I would've been about fourteen and I'd played in the grand final of our softball club competition. There was a party afterwards at the diamonds, organised by a girl called Kristy-Lee. She was a few years older than the rest of us and she was cool; we all looked up to her. She turned up to this end-of-season party with a bag full of UDLs, the sugary, sweet, premixed vodka drinks that teenagers across Australia begin their drinking careers with. Compared with Nonna's cheap wine, these went down the hatch nicely and I was soon feeling pretty good. I relaxed, I could chat to people without that voice in my head telling me what a weirdo I was, and I even started having a good time. Then something strange and miraculous happened. A boy called Dean, who I'd never met before, came along and sat down next to me on the grassy slope. I waited for him to insult me, because that's what boys in Stanthorpe usually did. But Dean was nice and he didn't seem to find me repulsive, which was a bonus. We chatted for a while, until suddenly I thought, 'Fuck it, here's my chance.'

I leaned over and before I even knew what was happening, I was having my first kiss. It was the most horrendous, disgusting washing-machine kiss you could imagine and it went on for what felt like bloody hours. But I was on top of the world: it had finally happened! Maybe I wouldn't be alone forever after all! I went home deliriously happy. But that was just the start — the next day, I woke up, looked in the mirror and discovered a hickie on my neck. A hickie! Miracle upon miracle! I could not believe my luck. I bounded off to school on Monday delighted to prove I was not the sexual pariah the other kids thought I was. I sat in art class with my shirt collar pulled as far down as possible, just dying for someone to notice. No one did, of course, because it was the tiniest, most pitiful excuse for a love bite in the history of love bites. But still. It was there, and I was on cloud fucking nine.

Years later, when I was in my first full-time job in radio at Sea FM on the Central Coast, my co-host Daniel Gawned and I decided to call the people with whom we'd had our first kisses and ask them for a review. I managed to track down Dean's number, phoned him live on air and asked: 'How was it for you?'

'Horrible,' was his recollection.

So long, Stanthorpe

'Brianna Tomasel has a penis! Brianna Tomasel has a penis!'

It was Grade 9, I was fourteen and the chants were ringing loud and clear across the corridor outside the classrooms at Stanthorpe State High. This kid had me cornered as I tried to make my way into class. He hated me because I was better at sport than him. Today, though, he seemed angrier than ever.

'Brianna Tomasel has a penis — that's why she's good at soccer, she's got a penis!' The boy was getting louder, and he was following me as I tried to get away from him.

'Leave me alone!' I yelled. He'd been picking on me for weeks, but this was the first time I actually felt scared of him. He was coming for me. Although he was a head shorter than me, the Danny DeVito of our grade, somehow he reached up and grabbed my shoulder. Before I could shake him off he brought his leg up and kneed me right between my legs. 'I'll prove she's got a penis,' he said, laughing as I keeled over and hit the ground. I'd never been hit in my vagina before, and my god it hurt. I lay on the ground, clutching my lady bits, which felt like they'd been smashed with a sledgehammer.

'See, I told you she's got a penis,' he told the crowd of kids who'd gathered around me. Some were pointing and laughing at me lying in a heap on the floor. Others just stood there. But no one said anything. No one asked if I was okay. And no one told that kid he was a dick, or that he should stop.

That was the push I needed. I couldn't deal with this shit anymore — I had to get out of there. I had to leave Stanthorpe State High and, actually, I wanted to get the fuck out of Stanthorpe altogether. I wanted to run as far away from those arseholes at school as I could. I would have got on a train that afternoon if there had actually been one.

One of my few good friends from softball had recently moved from her small town to a private boarding school in Brisbane, so I set my sights on doing the same. 'I want to go to boarding school,' I said over the dinner table that night.

'Don't be ridiculous, Brianna, you're not going to boarding school,' Mum said. 'Is she, Stephen? Back me up here. She's too young to go off and live away from home.'

Dad mumbled something non-committal. He didn't want to get in trouble with Mum, but I could see he thought it could be a good idea. He knew I wasn't happy at school and, besides, he'd gone to boarding school and loved it.

The way I convinced my parents was by focusing on the logistics. They (read: Mum) were spending close to twenty hours every week driving me to sports training, games and tournaments. Most weekends we were getting up at three or four in the morning to get me places. Mum never complained because she could see how happy sport made me, but the impact on the family was big. I had two other siblings who weren't getting anywhere near this kind of time and attention put into them.

Going to boarding school in Brisbane would solve that. Most of the sport would happen in the city and if I needed to travel, there would be public transport available. 'It just makes sense,' I told them, pretending I had no nerves at all over the prospect of moving away from home. On the inside, though, the thought of being away from Mum terrified me. I truly didn't have a clue how I could do life without her. But I knew there was no other option; I had to get away from Stanthorpe State High. Yeah, I was running from the bullies, but I was also running from myself. The older I got, the less comfortable I felt in who I was. I hoped a new environment would be the answer.

Mum and Dad finally agreed I could go when I was offered a scholarship at a private co-ed school called St Peters Lutheran College in Brisbane. I was lucky. The vice-principal was a former softballer and she wanted me on the school team because she thought I might help them win the super-competitive schools' competition. The scholarship would cover half my fees. It ended up being a good deal for the school, because St Peters did win the premiership every year for the three years I was there.

Mum says that the day I packed up and left home for St Peters was the worst day of her life. She felt like a piece of her heart was being torn out. Mum's a nurturer, and she certainly never imagined any of her kids would leave home at fifteen. As we drove out of Stanthorpe that morning, I didn't realise I would never live in that town again. I didn't realise I would never live in the same house as my parents again. Perhaps Mum had an inkling, though, which is why she cried for a solid three hours on the drive to Brisbane. Dad was driving and Mum was in the front seat next to him, while I was in the back squashed up against suitcases, pillows and sports gear ready for my new life. Mum kept turning around and asking 'Are you sure about this, Brianna? Are you sure this is what you want?'

Dad barely said a word. But when I stood on the steps of the main entrance to my new boarding house and waved them off, I saw Dad crying too. I was upset, sure — but I was also excited because this school was like a five-star hotel compared with the shithole school I'd come from. This place was flash! The school was made up of big brick buildings set on beautiful parklike grounds right in the heart of Brisbane. There were tennis courts, two huge swimming pools, a shiny new gym and three ovals. Boarders were spread across four boarding houses — two for girls and two for boys. I was put into Finger House. Yes, that's right — this all-girls dormitory was called Finger House. You have to wonder who was behind *that* decision.

Because I'd arrived mid-way through the year, the only

room left was a shitty little cubicle right by the front door. It was separated from the cubicle next door by a partition that didn't reach the ceiling and the door was actually a navy blue curtain. There was a single bed with a drawer underneath, a desk and a chair, and that was about it. I unpacked my stuff, put my Broncos posters up on the walls — a sweaty close-up of Darren Lockyer taking prime position over the head of my bed — and got on with the business of my new life.

It didn't take me long to realise that, unlike where I'd come from, this school had standards. Like, *high* standards. Our uniform of maroon blazer and tie and a maroon straw hat had to be worn correctly. Girls weren't allowed make-up (which obviously wasn't a problem for Tomboy Tomasel), hair had to be tied up and rules were to be obeyed. No chewing gum, no running in the hallways. There was a pride in the school, which rubbed off on the students. I was amazed to discover that at this school it was actually okay to try hard. It was a good thing to excel at something. For the first time in my life, being good at sport didn't mean there was a target on my back.

The weirdest thing about my new life, though, was that I wasn't the social outcast I'd been at home. On my first day, I found myself welcomed into the cool kids' group. 'There must be some mistake,' I felt like saying when I was called over and invited to join the circle of popular kids as they ate their lunch. In Stanthorpe, these types of kids either ignored me or mocked me. But at St Peters they seemed to like me, and — even better — over time I realised they found me funny.

SO LONG, STANTHORPE

* * *

There was something about the existence of rules at St Peters that made me want to bend them. I was ballsy and I had an audience, which turned out to be a killer combo. I started off slowly — you know, testing the waters with entry-level pranks like putting Vaseline on the handrail of the stairs and hiding from view to watch people go sliding. I wrapped the toilet seat with Glad wrap and tormented the young housemistresses whose job it was to look after us. 'Help, Miss Fox — Olivia's hurt herself,' I'd scream, making the poor mistress run the six floors down to the bottom of the stairs to find the girl I'd co-opted in a heap pretending to be dead. 'Hahaha just kidding,' we'd shriek, laughing our heads off as the mistress had to climb back up the six floors of stairs again.

It was stupid shit, but we were bored out of our brains a lot of the time so we did what we could to create our own entertainment. Once a bunch of us took an overdose of No-Doz — those caffeine pills truck drivers use to keep themselves awake — and we all went crazy. We didn't sleep for the entire weekend, instead making up a game where we jumped over the partitions that separated our cubicles. It was like two-metre-high hurdles. We'd clamber over, getting wedged up against the ceiling on the way before flopping down onto the bed... then on to the next one. There were so many of us that the mistresses couldn't get any control — we were like a pack of wild hyenas.

While I might have been good at sport and pranking, my

schoolwork was fast becoming a problem. At Stanthorpe State High, I did okay without even trying. Here, it became clear from day one how far behind I was academically. The work was hard and the expectations were high. I was out of my depth. I sat in class trying so hard to concentrate, but I struggled. And the less I understood what was going on, the more panicked I became. I felt anxious about the work, but no matter how much I wanted to study or get my assignments done, I couldn't seem to focus. I didn't even know where to start. I was made to sit at the front in class so the teachers could keep a close eye on me, and Mum and Dad ended up paying for a tutor to sit with me during study hour each evening to help me with my homework. Without the tutor, I was hopeless; I couldn't stay in my seat for more than five minutes. I was constantly looking around, jumping up and searching for others who might be keen to cause a bit of mischief. Even when it was a subject I liked, I found it so hard to focus long enough to get anything done.

I was also battling some pretty extreme homesickness. I called Mum every night on my piece-of-shit Nokia phone that I'd found on the oval at my old school. She would patiently listen to me sobbing down the phone. And she made the six-hour return trip every weekend to visit me.

At the start of Grade 11 we got a new boarding mistress, an American woman named Mrs Bond. Her job came with accommodation on-site, so she and her family moved in to a house directly opposite the boarding house and her three kids joined the school. Her oldest son, Liam, was in my class. This was a special class where they put kids like me who were playing sport at a high level. They called it the G&T class — not gin and tonic, sadly, but Gifted and Talented, which was a massive fucking joke because there was nothing gifted or talented about me, especially when it came to my schoolwork. But being in this class meant we got extra time for training, and we had fitness sessions, weights and stretching classes on top of our normal lessons. Doing this extra training meant we were excused from Christian Studies, which for me really was a gift from God.

As I was now sixteen, I felt it was high time to find myself a boyfriend so I focused my attention on Liam Bond. He was really good at AFL, so I noticed him straight away and decided he was cute. But because I was the world's most awkward teenager whose ugly-duckling phase seemed to be going on forever, I didn't say a word to him. Instead I stared at him when I thought he wasn't looking and daydreamed about him when I was supposed to be doing my schoolwork. But one night a friend had a party at her house, and thanks to the five glasses of Passion Pop sparkling wine I'd put away, I was feeling bold. I somehow made my way to Liam, who was as awkward as me, and made it clear I quite liked him — and hey presto, we ended up hooking up.

We pashed for hours at that party but on Monday at school we both went back to normal programming: pretending the other person didn't exist. This pattern continued for the rest of my time at St Peters. We'd hook up at the weekends and barely acknowledge each other during the week. We had to be careful to keep it a secret from his mum because we both knew I was definitely not the girl she would have chosen for her golden boy Liam. It's not that I was a bad kid, it's just that I was often getting into trouble. I was cheeky. And annoying. And I struggled to follow the rules of the boarding house. Because my room was right by the front door, I would hear when anyone was going in or out. Being easily distracted, I would leap up to see who it was, keen to wrangle others into my silly business. I got a reputation as a bit of a ringleader: Brianna Tomasel, CEO of Chaos.

The way security worked at the boarding house was that at night, the front doors automatically locked so that none of us could sneak out and no one could come in. But I, fancying myself as a bit of a George Clooney in *Ocean's Eleven*, figured out that if I shoved Blu-Tack into the lock, it wouldn't fully seal. This was quite the discovery because it meant I could now go between the boarding houses undetected after dark. I could sneak around and find other girls who were keen to muck around with me. It also meant I could scale the metal fence that separated my boarding house from the Bonds' and climb in through Liam's window. That was risky — if I'd got caught I would have been in extreme amounts of trouble, but somehow we managed to get away with it.

Mum and Dad were always getting calls from the school about the trouble I was getting up to. Once I decided it would be hilarious to unravel a fire hose that was mounted on the wall in a corridor. I dragged the hose into my friend Laura's room and pointed the nozzle at her like a gun. She looked me in the eye and said, 'Do it, I dare you.' She thought there was no way I'd be stupid enough to go through with it, but her dare was like a red rag to a bull. Without a second thought I pulled back the lever on the fire hose, the water firing out like a dam breaking. The pressure ripped the hose out of my hands and it flew around like a wild animal, drenching every surface and ruining everything in there. It was a complete soaking and we were screaming so loud that every girl in the boarding house — plus the mistresses and the matron, of course — came running.

I'd like to say I learned from my mistakes, but I did not. If I saw an opportunity for a laugh, I was almost incapable of thinking about the consequences. Most sixteen-year-olds weren't doing things like this, but the thrill of the gag and the risk element was intoxicating to me. I was a little shit, there's no doubt about that, but it was all pretty harmless stuff. I wasn't selling weed, stealing shit or bullying anyone. I just wanted to make people laugh.

As head of house, Mrs Bond was in charge of us and she had a team of house-mistresses who helped her. They were young women, usually university students, who lived at the boarding house for free and ate in the dining hall with us in exchange for working shifts at the school, where they supervised our study hour and kept an eye on us over the weekends. Some were awful and we combatted our boredom by tormenting them; others were cool, like Miss Sweeney. Miss Sweeney was about nineteen or twenty and was studying to become a school teacher. She wasn't a nerd like most of them and over time, she and I became friends. When she was on duty we would hang out. Every student at St Peters was aware that the mistresses each had a 'master key' — kind of like the key Willy Wonka had for his chocolate factory which could open every single door of the school. The library, the science labs, the principal's office, the swimming pool — and to us students it held a kind of magic. I used to joke with Miss Sweeney about how funny it would be if her key 'accidentally' found its way into my possession. She'd laugh along with me, but never in a million years did I think she'd do it.

Fast forward a few months and Miss Sweeney graduated from teachers' college and was no longer working at the boarding house. It was the end of term and I was in my room tidying up and packing to go home for the holidays. I picked a framed photo up off my desk and noticed something taped to the back of it. *No fucking way!* I knew immediately what it was and how it got there. Miss Sweeney, you *legend*.

I told a select group of girls about the key and we all swore to keep its existence a secret. We knew that the key, excuse the pun, to its success was ensuring word didn't get out. If it did, we were screwed and the newly minted teacher Miss Sweeney could be, too. That master key gave us a freedom we'd only dreamed of before. On weekends we could head out, do what we wanted, and let ourselves back in the front door at any hour of the night. One of my first missions was leading a contingent of girls out a side door to a party on a Saturday night. We carefully coordinated the timings to ensure there was no one patrolling the corridors, stuffed our beds with pillows to look like sleeping bodies, and snuck out quietly. After a few hours we headed back, letting ourselves back in with this glorious little key. There were security cameras, but I'd already worked out that if we crawled along on our hands and knees, we'd be out of view.

By the last year of school lots of us had cars, so coupled with the key it felt like freedom was finally within our reach. My parents bought me a Mitsubishi Mirage. It was a big-energy, girl-from-Queensland car, with real bogan vibes. Here's the best bit — it was harlequin purple! It had tinted windows, a custom-blue interior and a subwoofer in the boot. I *loved* it. When I turned the volume up to full, the car would shake so badly I couldn't see out the rear-view mirror. My days of catching buses and trains were over. I could go where I wanted when I wanted in the sickest car in Brissy.

* * *

My boarding school years were a mix of lows and highs. I was homesick a lot. I longed to be close to my family, and there were times when I wished I'd stayed back in Stanthorpe. When I was struggling with homework I'd think how lucky the day-kids were, the ones who could go home and get help with assignments. And when I got sick, there was no one else I wanted but Mum. One time I was on my death-bed with tonsillitis and had to walk 30 minutes to the doctor's — on my own — for antibiotics (the school had run out of taxi chits).

I was spending increasing amounts of time in the sick bay — a sad, sterile room by the school office with four hospital beds and a nurse keeping an eye on ill students and the ones who were faking. I wasn't faking anything. I'd end up in there on the first day of my period every month and would be stuck there until the next day. The pain was so awful that I couldn't stand up straight, and I felt so exhausted that I couldn't do anything but sleep. I was missing softball training and even games sometimes, which killed me. On those days I was so desperate to be at home with Mum taking care of me that I could hardly bear it. Later I found out I had polycystic ovaries and endometriosis, but it would take many more years of pain before I got those answers.

On the plus side, I had a little radio in my cubicle at boarding school. I listened to B105 breakfast radio with hosts Labby, Camilla and Stav. It was one of the most popular radio shows in Brisbane, and I loved those guys so much. The minute I woke up each morning, I'd turn on the radio. When I got back to my room in the afternoons, I'd flick it back on again. I didn't like silence, so having these guys chatting away and making me laugh made me feel okay. Labby's real name is Jason Hawkins, and in a weird twist he ended up becoming a mentor and a friend to me. It was Jase who convinced me to take the job in New Zealand. But back then, I hadn't yet started to dream about working in radio; I was just a devoted listener. I found their antics and their ability to entertain so bloody good. They did a thing called the Gotcha prank, where they set people up with fake phone calls, and another called The Fugitive, where they dropped someone on a random street in Brisbane and gave clues so that listeners could go out and find them. My friend Ali and I were obsessed with The

Fugitive — we'd spend entire days driving around searching, the car radio dropping little hints along the way.

I didn't know it at the time, but those early radio experiences as a listener — and a committed listener at that — shaped my own radio style so much. These guys were the ones who made me fall in love with radio. I loved the brilliant immediacy of radio and I could hear how much fun you could have on-air. I hadn't met these guys, I didn't even know what they looked like, but they were so authentic and so open that I genuinely felt like they were my friends.

I kissed a girl (and I liked it)

When I first started hooking up with my friend Gabby, it never occurred to me that kissing a girl might mean I was gay, lesbian, bisexual or anything else. It didn't cross my mind to put a label on myself or what we were getting up to, because I didn't feel strange or shameful at all. It felt, well, *natural* I guess. Don't you worry, a giant truckload of gay shame was headed my way, but at that point all I knew was I liked Gabby and it felt good to kiss her, so why not?

Gabby was far more than just a hook-up, though. She came into my life when I was about fifteen; we both played softball. Gabby was feisty like me, and we got on so well. She lived miles away from me, but we saw each other all the time because of our sport. When I moved to boarding school we texted constantly in that intense teenage way we all did. I'd buy a $30 credit to load on to my piece-of-shit Nokia, which I tried to make last as long as possible because I had fuck-all money. Each text cost 20 cents, so to save on credit Gabby and I did away with gaps between words, instead using capital letters at the start of each word:

HiGabbyHowAreYouIGotInSoMuchTroubleAt
SchoolTodayIWillCallTonightAndTellYouAboutIt

It was a dyslexic's nightmare but we got the hang of it. Included in my phone plan was unlimited calls between eight and nine each night, so I called that my Gabby hour. I'd phone her every night without fail and we'd talk for the full 60 minutes.

I leant on Gabby a lot, especially during those early days at boarding school when I was struggling with homesickness. I know it sounds weird, but I didn't notice my feelings changing from being just friends to something more — but when she came to stay in Stanthorpe during the holidays in my last year of school, we spent most of our time kissing on my little single bed. It felt great; way better than the average pashes I'd had with Liam Bond and the tiny handful of other boys who had miraculously come near me. Kissing Gabby felt right. We had such a tight friendship and close connection that this next step felt like a natural progression. Having said that, we knew instinctively that our hook-ups had to remain a secret. We agreed that if anyone found out, we'd be dead. If anyone had caught us in the act, I would have had to run away to the other side of the world and assume a new identity.

This layer of secrecy was completely different to what I'd done with my Liam fling. I'd spent hours debriefing with girls at school on exactly what he'd said, what it meant and what we'd got up to in his bedroom. But the idea of anyone finding out that I had kissed a girl was not an option. I still didn't know much about life, but I knew kissing girls wasn't 'normal'. In some ways, the secrecy aspect made our liaison even more fun. We knew we were up to something naughty and sneaking around behind our parents' backs became a bit of a game. One of the big perks of being a gay girl is being able to hide behind platonic friendships. What young girls don't enjoy a sleepover? Gabby and I certainly did. And I don't think my parents ever would've suspected we were anything other than good mates.

While we never would have described ourselves as each other's girlfriends, we really were in quite a serious relationship for most of my final year of school. We spoke every day, hooked up every time we were together, and she was my closest confidante. Gabby was the closest thing to a best friend that I'd ever had. I was stoked when we both ended up going to the University of Queensland. I was excited about living in the same place and naively assumed our relationship would continue as it was.

For the first few weeks, things were great. We spent heaps of time together, hanging out and hooking up in my little room with its single bed and thin walls at the student housing where

I lived with 100 other teenagers. We finally had total freedom to do whatever we wanted, with no one checking up on us, and we were determined to make the most of it. But then, Gabby started to change towards me. I would suggest hanging out and she always had an excuse. I'd message her and she wouldn't text back.

'What's going on?' I asked her, after it became clear she was avoiding me.

'Nothing,' she insisted.

I persisted, but she wouldn't talk to me or even acknowledge that there had been anything special between us at all. She made out like I'd invented the whole thing. I felt so confused, and totally heartbroken. It wasn't just the loss of our romantic relationship — she was also my best friend, and all of a sudden she'd gone cold on me. I felt incredibly lonely.

After months of asking Gabby for answers, I gave up. It's only now, fifteen years on, that I think I've worked out what happened. She must have been terrified that her new friends would find out about me, about our relationship. And, like most teenagers, she just wanted to be normal and to be like everyone else. Let's face it: hooking up with girls wasn't normal, was it? So she pushed me away and got on with a life that didn't include me. I had no choice but to get on with mine, too, but I was sad for a long time after that. The worst thing was that because it was all such a big secret, I had no one to talk to about it.

* * *

After Anna Kournikova, my next big crush was Christina Aguilera. You know — Christina in her 'Dirrty' era, when she sported piercings, dirty dreads and arse-less leather chaps while grinding around in a sweaty boxing ring? I was obsessed with that single. And when she released *Stripped*, I listened to that back-to-back probably 2000 times. My CD got scratches on it from the excessive use, and by the end I knew exactly where in which songs it was going to jump, and I'd just sing along, skips and all.

When she toured the *Stripped* album I didn't even bother asking my parents if I could go. 'You're too young for a concert like that,' Mum would have said. But a few years later, when I was eighteen, she toured again. I was living in Brisbane and nothing would have kept me away. I used every last cent I could scrape together to get a ticket. A big group of my friends also wanted to go, but I didn't trust that they'd get good enough tickets. So I was like, 'You guys go ahead, I'm going to pay for the best seats money can buy. I'll just catch up with you after the show.' I wasn't worried about going alone; I just wanted to get up close and personal to Christina. This is how much of a psycho I was. I bought a single ticket as close to the stage as I could find. I was so pumped. But when I turned up on the night, I was in the fourth row back, all by myself — only to look up and see my mates taking their seats two rows in front of me! I felt like such a loser.

Despite my relationship with Gabby and my obsessive crushes on hot women like Anna Kournikova and Christina

Aguilera, I still didn't think of myself as queer. And I didn't think I wasn't queer, either. I just didn't spend much time thinking about it. In my experience, it's usually straight people who want to know what it is I am. Bisexual? Maybe. Sexually fluid? I guess. Why did I have to have a name for what I was? I wasn't straight, that's for sure. Couldn't I just be me?

After Gabby went cold on me, I dealt with my loneliness and heartbreak in the best way I knew how — hitting the clubs in a big way. I was tearing up that D-floor and I was ready to mingle with pretty much anyone who'd give me the time of day. I was open to flings with guys, although truth is, boys were still not that into me. Too big, too tall, too loud, too opinionated, too funny . . . I don't know what it was, but I could count on one hand the number of guys who'd liked me. When it came to girls, though, it was a different story: I had much more luck attracting women. And here's my theory on that. In the straight pool, I would say I'm a solid 5 out of 10 in the looks department. In the gay pool, I shoot up to a 7 out of 10, maybe even 8 on a good day. The lesbian community is a smaller pool, you see. There are slimmer pickings, so it's easier to stand out. This means that being a 7 out of 10 in the lesbian world gives me access to other high-rankers. If I were solely trying to meet straight men, I'd be stuck with other 5-ers. So what I'm getting at here is that it's not a hard choice for me on which way to go. I can get the beat-up old Corolla or the hot yellow V12 Lamborghini.

I did actually lose my straight virginity eventually, to a poor, unsuspecting boy called Tom. It was such an underwhelming experience that it did nothing to convince me to give boys another shot anytime soon. Sorry, Tom, but I was getting the distinct impression that for all its hype, sex with boys wasn't very exciting. The whole encounter felt so different to what I'd shared with Gabby.

* * *

For all you straight people out there who might not know this, the sport of softball is a global lesbian hotbed. You want to meet girls? Join your local softball team. When I made the Under 19 Queensland softball team I was suddenly surrounded by women having relationships with other women. I'd opened the door to a world I didn't know existed, but I quite liked the look of it.

Pretty soon I started dating a girl in the team called Maya. She was a year younger than me, just seventeen, and still at school. Even though we were in a really supportive environment in terms of same-sex relationships, we decided to keep ours a secret. We didn't want to be part of the gossiping that was going on around us and the judgement from coaches and parents that we'd picked up on. Most importantly, though, Maya's mum was Indian and, like my Catholic dad, had been vocal about her views on homosexuality. Neither Maya or I had any interest in opening *that* can of worms.

But I couldn't ignore the fact that I was clearly attracted to women and I finally started to think about what that meant for me. Also, what did it mean *about* me? Being gay was wrong, wasn't it? I felt safe when I was surrounded by all these amazing women in my softball team. But the minute I thought about going home to Stanthorpe and seeing my family, I felt sick. 'What if they find out?' I thought. 'What if they look at me and can see I'm different to them?' My feelings were a mix of curiosity and excitement about this new world I was in, and a touch of disappointment that I had turned out this way. I thought more than once that life would have been a hell of a lot easier if I could have just been into boys.

I knew in my heart that my family must never find out about this side to me. I would do everything I could to keep it hidden. I didn't realise it then, but this was the start of a double life for me. In Brisbane I could be myself, but in Stanthorpe there were parts of me that had to stay locked away. Dad's comments about poofters and gays were ringing in my ears. I knew *exactly* where he stood on homosexuals. He didn't like them. And I knew why; the Church had told him that people like me were wrong. That homosexuals were sinners. And we all knew where sinners ended up, and it wasn't in heaven.

This made me question the strength of Dad's love for me. Would he disown me if he found out? I decided he probably wouldn't, because Mum wouldn't let him. But would he still love me in the same way? I doubted it. Would he be able to rethink his religious views? I wasn't sure. Would he be disgusted by his own daughter? Highly likely. Would he be ashamed of me? Yes, I believed he would — and that broke my heart.

I rationalised my relationship with Maya as being about exploring who we were. There wasn't necessarily a huge spark between us, but it was nice to have someone to be curious with. We ended up dating for about six months, but when the softball season ended, so did the relationship. Things just fizzled out. And, keeping 'us' a secret had also become a burden. The seeds of shame were growing and I couldn't shake the sense that we were, somehow, doing something wrong.

After Maya, I went back to hooking up with boys. While in the softball world it was okay to hook up with girls, at Raymont Lodge all I could see were straight kids. So I would go out, drink lots, and end up pashing different guys. I never formed an actual relationship with any of them — as far as I was concerned, it was all just a bit of fun.

The Beat goes on

Uni was not necessarily the best choice for me, but when I'd got to the end of high school I'd had no idea what to do with my life. Most of the kids I knew were going to university, so I blindly followed. And because sport was the only thing I was good at, I enrolled in an exercise physiology degree. Along with all the other kids in Raymont Lodge, an old brick building on campus, I was feverish with excitement about having freedom for the first time in my life.

Sending a person like me — with, I learned later, undiagnosed ADHD — into that environment without any support was a recipe for disaster. There were a lot of issues. Firstly, a huge lecture hall filled with 300 people was not a place where I could learn anything. I couldn't follow what the lecturer was droning on about — I was distracted by every sound, shuffle, whisper and cough. I stared at the ceiling, doodled in my book, listened to the millions of thoughts bombarding my brain and checked my phone every ten seconds. Tutorials were a bit easier, with just 30 kids in the class, and I had more success there; but my commitment levels left a lot to be desired. It turned out that I didn't give a shit about the science of sport or how the human body worked. Total snore fest.

Independence caused other issues. At boarding school I'd had teachers and house-mistresses breathing down my neck and making sure I got my work done. Here I was a free agent. There was no one forcing me to turn up to my lectures and tutorials. There was no one making sure I didn't stay out too late, and no one holding my hand as I cried my way through assignments. And it was clear that, left to my own devices, I was a disaster. My marks were bloody terrible.

While academically I was fucked, socially I was thriving! This period of my life saw the beginning of my partying era, where going out was the best fun in the world. I don't know how I did it, but it wasn't unusual for me to be out drinking four or five nights a week. And I'm not talking a civilised glass or two of chardonnay; I'm talking beers, cheap nasty wine, vodka Red Bulls, Jägerbombs, shots of god knows what . . . I was putting away more booze than any human body should have been able to handle. I'd get about three hours of sleep and wake up the next morning looking like death and smelling worse, but ready to do it all again. (Of course, when my doctor enquired about my alcohol intake I gave the old 'one to two standard units a week' answer. We all do that, right?)

Almost without fail I would end up at The Beat Megaclub,

the greatest place on earth. The Beat is an absolute icon on the Brisbane queer scene. It's Australia's longest-running club, apparently having started off as a one-room gay bar and dance floor in the '80s and growing into what it is today: a seething, heaving, sweaty mammoth of a nightclub that turned out to be the first place I ever felt truly comfortable in. It was a safe space for the LGBTQI+ community and the only place where I felt accepted, loved and not judged.

Inside this massive club were five separate nightclubs, all playing different types of music and attracting different types of people. There was the trance room, where hardcore ravers danced in their reflective flared pants. Then there was the Wreckers room, which played R&B and hip-hop and was always one of my favourites. The pop room played banger after banger. Kylie Minogue, Cascada, all the classics. It was the smallest and hottest of the rooms, filled with hundreds of sweaty bodies dancing together like their lives bloody depended on it. And then there was the stripper room, with a shiny silver pole in the middle of the dance floor and people getting up to god knows what around it. I climbed it once. It didn't end well.

Dotted around this glorious maze of a place were seven bars, where we'd push through the crowd to shout our drinks orders over the thumping noise. We'd start with a couple of Smirnoff Ice Double Blacks topped up with raspberry to help it go down a bit easier. If we needed to ramp things up, we'd have an ABC shot — a disgusting mix of absinthe, Bacardi 151 and Chartreuse. It was horrendous, but if you could keep it down it would seriously put a rocket up your arse. Sometimes I'd need to whip into the loo for a 'tac yak' or tactical vomit; a quick spew before getting straight back out there and ordering another drink.

Most bizarrely, right in the middle of this amazing wonderland of fun was a greasy little tuck shop that sold hot chips and Chiko Rolls. If you're an Aussie you'll know what ChikoRolls are. For those who don't, they're disgusting deep-fried pastry tubes filled with cabbage and beef and other unidentifiable mush. They're like a cross between a spring roll and a pie, and the absolute perfect way to end a night at The Beat. We'd fall out of there at 5 a.m., clutching our delicious Chiko Rolls, bleary-eyed, sweaty and reeking of booze, and make our way home through the deserted Brisbane streets, yelling and singing and feeling like life couldn't get much better. I never got tired of it.

I know it's ridiculous to say that this dingy old nightclub in Fortitude Valley in Brisbane became my second home. But it did, because at The Beat I could be whoever I wanted to be. The way it made me feel must be the way straight people feel everywhere. The Beat was a welcoming and open place for humans of every bloody variety. Gay ones, straight ones, trans ones, drunk ones, sober ones; it didn't matter who the hell you were once you walked through those doors, everyone was accepted. And everyone in there was tied together because at The Beat we could be our authentic selves. We all lived in a society that told us we shouldn't be this way, that our lives were going to be harder, and that we were weird or wrong for who we were. But at The Beat, all that melted away. Every hangover I got from that place was worth it.

THE BEAT GOES ON

* * *

I can only describe the following two years as a hot mess. I was lost — I was running from who I was and terrified of adulthood. I'd bailed out of uni but I didn't have a clue in hell about what I wanted to do next or where I wanted to be. I needed to work out who I was and what I wanted to be, so in the meantime I bounced around carefree with zero responsibilities and for most part, had a pretty good time. I moved to America for 18 months on a softball scholarship, I went home to Stanthorpe for a couple of months, and I picked up part time jobs here and there. Notable mentions include a stint in a lettuce factory packing mesclun before another highly mentally-stimulating role, this time packing those little slices of apple kids get in a McDonald's Happy Meal. Both jobs involved the same uniform of hair net, white dungarees and abattoir-style gumboots. Sexy.

I was going out loads and having fun, but you've probably got the picture I was on a runaway train to nowhere. After a while, this lifestyle grew a bit tired and I knew I could and should be doing more. I am a super ambitious person and it was time to get out there and start achieving something again.

Deep down, I knew what I wanted to do. It was the dream I'd never said out loud for fear of jinxing it. I'd barely even admitted it to myself.

I wanted to be on the radio.

There, I said it. I wanted to be like Labby, Camilla and Stav, those guys whose voices kept me company at boarding school.

They were the ones who planted the seed that maybe I could have a career entertaining people and making them laugh. The more I thought about it, the more determined I was. Now I just had to figure out how to make it happen.

I found a flat in Brisbane, went back to the University of Queensland, and enrolled in a Bachelor of Communications, Public Relations and Journalism. I got a part-time job on the front desk at Thrifty Car Rental to help pay my way, and buckled in for four years of my least favourite thing — study. I wasn't totally stupid; I knew that if anyone was going to give me a chance in radio, I had to knuckle down and get this degree. I hated every second of it. But somehow, I got through it and graduated with solidly average marks. Cs get degrees, people.

Everyone else on the course seemed jazzed by the idea of PR and journalism — the class was full of pretty, well-put-together girls desperate to be like Samantha from *Sex and the City* with a job in PR and a great wardrobe. I, however, was not. If I'm honest, I still don't really know what PR is, other than helping people avoid being cancelled. From the very start, I only had eyes for commercial radio. And I knew that if I was going to get my ass anywhere near it, I needed some experience. So, halfway through my final year, I walked into the student radio station office on campus and asked if they had any work experience going. I offered to do anything — I would've swept floors and scrubbed the toilets if that's what they'd needed. But amazingly, they asked if I'd like to host a one-hour slot on-air on Tuesday afternoons.

OMG — I GOT MY OWN RADIO SHOW!!!

Well, sort of. It was more of an internet broadcast than a proper radio frequency, and obviously since it would be on a Tuesday afternoon when students were all in lectures there would be literally no one listening. But I didn't give a shit. I knew I had a guaranteed audience of one (Mumma Di) and that was enough for me. I felt like I'd hit the fucking jackpot.

After a twenty-minute lesson on which buttons to push and when, it was time for my radio debut. I'd never been so nervous in my life. Ten minutes in, Mum texts me: 'You're doing so well, Brianna! I'm loving it!'

That was a barefaced lie. It was the most amateur attempt at broadcasting in the history of broadcasting. A four-year-old would have done a better job. But I didn't care. The buzz of being live on radio and creating the playlist and deciding what to say was the best feeling I'd ever had. For that one hour each week, I felt more focused than I ever had. I wanted to do well in a way I'd never felt off the sports field. I realised I had found my thing.

* * *

Towards the end of the degree, students had to decide if they wanted to do an internship at a workplace, and if so, where. I sent off a bunch of emails to all the big radio stations in Brisbane asking if they had opportunities for work experience and offering to work in any role for free. Of course, me being me, I'd left it really late to apply for an internship, so I got a 'thanks but no thanks' from most of the stations as they'd already filled their positions. I had almost given up hope when an email popped up in my inbox from someone at Nova 106.9 — one of the biggest radio stations — saying that while they didn't have room for more interns, they did need some help for a few weeks.

'Would you like to come in for an interview?'

Yes — yes I would! A few days later I was walking into the coolest workplace I'd ever seen. Nova was housed in a big converted brick warehouse and it was everything I could have dreamed of. Exposed beams, industrial lights, a ping-pong table and cool young people everywhere . . . it felt like I was in a movie-set radio station. I remember thinking 'This is so fucking awesome.'

I can't remember who interviewed me or what I was asked about, but a couple of days later I got the most exciting email of my life: 'Hey Bree, we'd love you to come in and do some experience.' I would be working (for free, of course) behind the scenes of a Nova Breakfast Show promotion called Nova's Got Balls. My first day was spent in a windowless room blowing up 4000 beach balls for eight hours straight. There was no pump or anything like that, just me and my breath for eight hours. And I am not kidding when I say I loved every minute of it — because I knew I was a very tiny part of something big and fun and exciting. Who knew all my hot air would come in handy one day?

The following day was when the real excitement began,

though. I met the rest of the team at a park on Brisbane's South Bank at 4 a.m., where the big event was taking place. I was a minion helping with the set-up, and my job was to empty the 4000 beach balls into a giant ball pit, lug sandbags into place, put up flags and make sure everything was ready to go. The listeners who'd won a place in the draw arrived, the Breakfast hosts were setting up for their live broadcast from the park, and joggers and walkers were stopping to see what was going on.

Everyone in the draw had to get into the pit and collect balls to put into a big sack in the allocated amount of time. Each ball had a number written on it (by me, of course!) and the person who got the winning number won $50,000. There was such a buzz of excitement and energy that even though I was a tiny minion at the absolute bottom of the food chain, I didn't care. I was fizzing at the bunghole just being part of something so cool and I couldn't believe people got to call this their actual job.

At one point during the morning, I saw a guy from Nova called Scotty Couchman who seemed to be struggling a bit with the balls while trying to do something else at the same time. I didn't even think about it; I went up to him and said 'Here, I'll hold these and hand them to you when you need them.' It didn't seem like a big deal, but I later found out he told the boss: 'We need to keep that girl Bree, she's good.'

And at the end of my four weeks of work experience, my mind was blown when I was offered a permanent role on the Nova street team. They told me that Scotty had played a big part in this — he believed I had what it took to work there. I'd never have guessed that handling a guy's balls with care would have got me a job in radio, but here we were! The street team organised all the events and activations around the city. It was all about promotion and engagement. The role certainly didn't involve me being anywhere close to a microphone, but I knew it was an extremely important step in the right direction. I couldn't have been happier.

* * *

Something strange happened during those first few weeks at Nova. For the first time in my life, I felt like I'd found my people. Everywhere else — high school, university, back home in Stanthorpe — I had the sense that I didn't fit in, that I was weird and out of place. Here though, in the radio world, I felt at home.

During my work experience, Scotty must have known how obsessed I was with the whole business of radio. I was a radio nerd. I wanted to know how it all worked and how every part of this big, fun machine came together. Scotty offered to take me on a tour of the air lock. This is the area in a radio station where the broadcasting happens. It is the most important part of the building, accessed through massive, heavy, sound-proofed doors. I couldn't contain my excitement, seeing this for the first time; I was in awe as Scotty walked me down the corridor. I looked through the windows into each studio, where the radio people were on-air. The idea that those guys with their headphones on in front of their microphones and buttons were connecting with thousands of people gave me the feels. I knew it was where I needed to end up. I just had to work out how to get there.

The weird thing is, for all the insecurities and anxieties that plagued every other part of my life, I knew I could make it in radio. I just knew I could do it. There was never a back-up plan, never anything else I wanted to do, so making it work wasn't a matter of 'if'. I simply *had* to succeed. I was continually surprised by this unfamiliar self-belief when it came to radio. I don't know where it came from, because it didn't extend to much else in my life. I didn't think I was a particularly great person, I felt massively confused about who I was, and there was a part of me that felt shameful and wrong. But when it came to my future career — I was going to be on the radio, and that was that. I've always been uncomfortable about tooting my own horn, but this time I knew I had the determination to give it everything. When I'm passionate about something I'll work my arse off, and I would have sacrificed everything else in my life to do what I needed to do to make it in radio.

You have to be funny on radio, that's true, but there's so much more to it than that. You have to be creative, smart, relatable, adaptable and quick on your feet. Surely I ticked at least a couple of those boxes?! I already knew I was good at making people laugh — I had always used humour as a way to cope with all the shit going on in my head, and I was good at it. The idea of bringing a bit of light and laughter into people's days made me so happy. I couldn't think of anything better than getting to do that for a job. I thought that if I could make entertaining people my job, I would never work a day in my life. Which turned out not to be true at all: radio is bloody hard work. But there is an amazing payback because when it goes well, there is no better feeling than knowing you've made a difference to someone's day.

* * *

Working in Nova's street team was a mixture of incredible fun and absolute exhaustion. I was in such a head space of 'I have to make it' that I was pushing myself to the absolute brink, working fourteen-hour days six and sometimes seven days a week, saying yes to absolutely everything that came along. I was convinced that people around me thought a country girl like me couldn't make it in radio and that drove me even harder.

But while I had that self-belief about being on-air, sadly it didn't come with a side-serving of instant talent. My first attempt at an aircheck did not go well. An aircheck is a demo recording, which anyone who wants a chance at being on-air must do to prove they're any good. I worked hard on mine, going into the studio on my own time for months, and thought it was sounding okay. But when I took it to the programme director, Jay Walkerden, for a listen, he didn't beat around the bush.

'Are you sure this is what you want to do? You really want to work in radio?'

'Yes, definitely,' I said.

'Well, you've got a lot of work to do, because that was terrible.'

Wow, that took me down a few pegs. But you know what? He was right. My aircheck was terrible. And to be honest, I'm still a pretty average solo announcer. I've come to realise I perform best with a sidekick; I love having someone to bounce off. It's collaboration that brings out the best in me.

Jay's response left me deflated, thinking 'Where the hell do I go from here?' But as I had no back-up career plan, I had no choice but to keep on going. The weekend rolled around and there I was, back in the studio in my own time practising again because, well, obviously I needed it.

After several months in the street team, I was spending every weekend at the studio too. There were fewer people around on Saturdays and Sundays, so I would offer to lend a hand with anything that needed doing. After a while, I put together a slightly less terrible aircheck and was given the opportunity to be on-air occasionally. It wasn't every weekend and it wasn't a lot, but I grabbed every chance I got. I fucking *loved* it. I came alive on-air — it's where I felt happiest. I spent my downtime thinking of ways to create great content, and the rest of the time hanging around the studios looking for opportunities to prove myself.

In the end, it was a nudie-run through the office by my mate Daniel 'Gawndy' Gawned that sealed the deal. Gawndy was a seasoned radio guy and he'd taken me under his wing. For a year or so we'd been putting demos together, begging the bosses to give us a chance as a double-act. We called our hypothetical show 'pop-up radio' because we were offering to pop up on-air anytime they needed us. Eventually, Jay said he'd give us our own weekend show if Gawndy did a lap of the office naked. He didn't think twice — stripped off, grabbed a garden gnome off Jay's desk to hide his meat-and-two-veg and off he went. The girls in sales didn't know where to look, but Gawndy didn't care. Once again, who would have thought a guy's balls would have got me my big break?

Nabbing the weekend breakfast show was a huge deal to me, but it didn't mean I could quit my day job. I didn't think twice about working seven days a week, though, because I was finally doing what I'd dreamed of.

Gawndy and I were mates and we got on well, but it took a while for us to find our feet with the show and it was a bit wobbly at the start. We both had big personalities, were super-ambitious and, looking back, it took a bit of time for us to figure out our roles. I was learning fast that a radio partnership is only successful if each host is prepared to help the other shine. Gawndy taught me the importance of throwing balls in the air for your co-host to grab — if you don't work together like that, and instead only focus on yourself, the show is doomed from the start.

We soon found our rhythm and loved working together. Our ratings were going up and we were getting a bit of a following. I couldn't believe that after dreaming about doing this for so long, it was finally bloody happening.

Lesbian-ish

By my early twenties I was hanging around with a group of girls who I would describe as 'lesbian-ish'. Some were loud-and-proud wave-your-rainbow-flag out-as-out-could-be, while others were still at the exploring-who-they-were stage. One thing we all had in common, though, was an openness to being whoever the hell you wanted to be. Every Tuesday we would meet up at the Paddington Hotel, a dingy, blokey kind of pub right near Suncorp Stadium. It was the unofficial Broncos supporters' bar, but on Tuesday nights we were lured in by $10 jugs of beer and a karaoke machine.

The ringleader of this gang of girls was Shaz, and she was your classic lesbian. You know: short hair, leather jacket, and the all-important item every lesbian must have in their lesbian starter-pack: a vest. You know: an Aladdin-style waistcoat — this bitch looked liked she'd just flown in from gay Agrabah on her magic rug-munching carpet. Shaz was real confident in herself. But she was also super-cute and really cool and she took us younger ones under her wing. Looking back, I think she must have been a small-time drug dealer — nothing serious, a bit of weed here and there — because she always had pockets full of cash. One night, we were all as drunk as sin and we went back to Shaz's house after the Paddo. There we were, about ten of us in her room lying on her bed having drinks, when she decided to start making bets with people. It was truth or dare with cash rewards. I was lying next to my friend Temica, who I'd known for a few years through softball. She was three years younger than me but we'd become real good mates.

'I dare you to kiss Temica for 30 seconds,' Shaz said, filming us on a handicam video camera she pulled out from the drawer in her bedside table. The group cheered as we leant in and kissed for the assigned 30 seconds. That was the easiest $20 I'd ever made.

The next day Temica sent me a text. 'Hahahaha how fucking funny was last night! Like how ridiculous, in what world would you and I end up kissing each other?' I sent back a few hahaha's and thought nothing more of it. Our lesbian-ish gang broke up and went our separate ways for the Christmas holidays — going home to our families where most of us pretended we were not lesbian-ish at all.

In the new year it was my twenty-first birthday, so I organised a big party at The Beat. Where else, right? I threw back a shit-ton of Double Blacks and was feeling real loose when I saw that Temica had arrived. I ran over to give her a hug, but the look on her face stopped me in my tracks. She looked super stressed-out and upset.

'What's happened? Are you okay?'

'Not really,' she said. 'I need to talk to you.'

Uh oh. I was too pissed to deal with a crisis, but she pulled me away into the corner of a room where we sat down. She looked absolutely petrified, which was weird because Temica was usually totally confident. I had no idea what she was about to tell me.

'You know, since that night we hooked up . . . I've realised I've got feelings for you and I can't get you out of my head.'

Ah shit. I was so drunk, I just sat there and said nothing. I didn't want drama on my twenty-first birthday! So I did the mature thing: I stood up and ran away, disappearing into the crowded dance floor. I managed to avoid Temica for the rest of the night. The next night, I dragged my hungover self to the pub to meet my friend Stacy. Another drink was the last thing my battered liver needed, but self-regulation has never been my strong point. And besides, Stacy had brought a friend along, an English girl called Dani. Dani was hot. Like seriously hot. She had long brassy blonde hair, a nice tan, a half-sleeve tattoo on her arm and these amazing, striking blue eyes. We sat at the bar drinking Coronas and talking. We talked and we talked and we talked. I liked Dani. She was super-charismatic and her London accent was the cherry on top. In an ideal world, Stacy would have picked up on our vibes and left me and Dani to it, but she was loving this get-together as much as us and despite our ridiculously unsubtle flirting, she wasn't going anywhere. We all ended up back at my house and the only way we could get rid of her was sending her out to Maccas for chicken nuggets.

Before long, Dani and I were together. And I was happy. She was uncomplicated and funny. People used to comment on how we were so similar, and it's true; sometimes it felt like we were twins. It was a lovely relationship because it was fun and effortless, with no drama. And mainly we made each other laugh.

But bubbling away in the background for the six months Dani and I were in a relationship was the Temica dilemma, which of course hadn't gone away. It was a tricky dynamic because she was still one of my best friends and we were hanging out, but she couldn't let go of her feelings for me. She couldn't believe I'd hooked up with Dani and she wouldn't drop that kiss we'd had. She loved a deep and meaningful, but I wasn't interested. I became a master of dodging and weaving the topic of 'us' whenever she brought it up.

I know this is making Temica sound like a Stage Five Clinger, which isn't actually fair. It was me running from this undeniable connection. We both knew it was there, but because of my internal battles I couldn't handle it. I wasn't ready.

In the end, Dani had to head back to the UK so our relationship had run its course. I knew I finally had to face with what was going on with Temica. And I realised I'd been dodging her because I didn't know how to do a proper relationship. I couldn't face the idea of a serious relationship because I knew my Brisbane life would eventually collide with my Stanthorpe one. I was also worried about my friendship with Temica being ruined in the same way it had happened with Gabby. That was the last thing I wanted.

I wrestled with my feelings for a long time, doing what I'm best at — lying awake worrying about hypothetical situations that would probably never happen. Finally, I texted Temica. 'You better come over because we need to talk.'

She turned up on my doorstep, and the moment we saw each other we knew it was all on. We were a couple. And things got serious, like *really* serious, pretty fast. I felt bad for what I'd put Temica through but it was what I needed to work things out. By the time Temica and I got together, I had absolutely no doubts about us. And when the lease was up on the house I was living in, Temica and I moved in together. We found a three-bedroom place with no aircon — a fucking nightmare in Brisbane — and our friend Tash moved in, too. I was just 21, Temica was only 19, but we were in love! And it was great; it was great for a really long time.

* * *

Temica was fully open about our relationship and her parents were cool about it, which felt amazingly liberating — at that point, I had no intention of ever revealing that side of my life to my family. The truth about me and Temica was easy to hide because our place had three bedrooms, so as far as I was concerned my parents never needed to know that we shared a room. My double life was in full swing. In Brisbane, I could be myself. At home in Stanthorpe, I had to pretend.

'Have ya found a boyfriend yet, Brianna?' Dad would ask when I went home to visit.

'No Dad, not yet, I'm still looking.'

HA HA. It was so fun playing straight with my parents, I really loved it. It made me feel so good about who I was and the web of lies I was unwittingly spinning around myself. NOT. I fucking LOATHED it. I'm not a liar, and living dishonestly like this made me feel like shit.

As time went on, Temica started putting pressure on me to be honest with my family about us. She couldn't understand how I could be so close to my parents yet so scared of what they might think about me. 'What are you ashamed of?' she asked. 'Just tell them, it'll be fine, they're lovely people!'

'They *are* lovely people, but you're not Catholic and you're not Italian — you don't get it,' I'd say. I wasn't ready to face the judgement. I didn't think I'd ever be ready. But the secret was getting harder to keep. Logistically it was easy because we were pretending to be just flatmates. But the emotional burden was growing, and I noticed I was getting increasingly angry and resentful. I was annoyed I couldn't just be normal like Amber and Aden, who were always taking their latest boyfriends and girlfriends home to the farm. Mostly I was angry at Dad. I was angry that I couldn't trust him to still love me if he found out I was queer.

I didn't want to ever tell my family, but Temica was on me

like a rash about it almost every day. And I think this is one of the hardest things about same-sex relationships — often each person is at a very different stage in their journey. One might be out and proud, like Temica was, while the other is still wrestling with the heaviness of secrets and shame. That's a stressful blend, and can mean you're in and out of the closet depending on who you're dating. Some relationships are light and fun because the person you're with doesn't carry baggage, while others feel like a great, big dirty secret, because what you're doing feels so shameful and so wrong that you have to operate carefully and secretively. That is not a fun way to live. All it does is further cement the internalised shame that sits in the pit of your stomach.

Temica was right, though — the secrecy couldn't go on. I think she'd noticed my stress was building about this double life I'd created. Things between us were getting heavy because the topic of coming out to my family had begun dominating our conversations. I had no intention of ever telling Dad, Amber or Aden, but finally agreed I'd tell Mum. Mumma Di is my number one fan. Even though I felt embarrassed revealing this side of myself to her, I knew she would continue to support me and love me.

But because I'm a giant pussy, I delivered the news by text.

'Mum, I need to tell you something.'

'What is it, Brianna?'

'I'm dating Temica.'

My phone rang almost as soon as I'd pressed send. It was Mum, of course, and she wanted to talk. I can't remember exactly what she said, but she was kind and supportive, and she tried to act like this was NO BIG DEAL. But it *was* a big deal and I felt like she was being a bit naive. I don't think she'd ever even met a gay person before, let alone one who was her daughter. She was trying to act like everything was normal, but she had loads of questions and that annoyed me. 'How long have you had these sorts of feelings? When did the relationship develop? Do you think it's just a phase?'

These were questions Amber and Aden would never face, and that pissed me off. It wasn't Mum's fault; it was just another part of the exhausting reality of falling outside of 'normal'. I felt super-awkward and clammed up. I didn't want to talk to her about this anymore. In my mind I was thinking, 'Okay, that's done. I'll never have to talk about that again.'

But here comes the bit I regret more than anything. She asked if I wanted her to tell Dad and I said no. In fact I shouted no. I begged and pleaded with her not to tell him or anyone else, ever in her life. Mum didn't try to talk me round. She didn't say, 'Dad will accept this, Dad will still love you the same.' Instead she said: 'Okay Brianna, I promise.'

And Mum agreeing to keep this from Dad confirmed my biggest fear — that he wouldn't love me the same way if he found out. I wondered if Mum was afraid of this, too. Maybe she was trying to protect me because she couldn't have been sure of his response, either.

So that was that, I'd come out to my mum. But I wasn't flooded with relief the way some people are when the secret is finally out. And it didn't feel as good as I'd hoped. Maybe that's because I'd only half shared it.

I didn't realise that asking Mum to keep it a secret would become one of the biggest regrets of my life. I was only 21. I was just muddling my way through this, but, my god, I really wish I'd just told everyone straight away and avoided the next decade of secrets and shame.

* * *

Not long afterwards, Temica and I broke up. It's taken years of reflection for me to figure out what went wrong, but I know now it was my fault. I sabotaged that relationship because I could see a future with Temica. That terrified me because being in a serious relationship meant I couldn't continue to explain what I was doing as 'a bit of fun' or 'just exploring'. Staying with Temica meant I would have to own up to who I really was. It would have meant saying goodbye to the old version of me — the one who could keep pretending who she was to her family.

Temica was my first true love, and I will always regret hurting her. I couldn't get past my own shit and allow myself to actually be happy, and she was the casualty in it all.

Menty-B #1

'Are you okay, Bree?' asked Gawndy. 'You don't seem yourself.' I'd just come off-air from our weekend show on Nova. I thought I'd done okay — I'd had years to practise hiding my rampant anxiety from everyone around me. But maybe the mask was slipping.

I was unravelling. Falling apart. I knew I was in a bad way, but I didn't quite realise yet where I was headed. 'Nah, I'm okay. Honestly.'

What a liar. I was fucked. Why didn't I just admit I needed help? For weeks I'd been feeling weird, like I was operating outside of my body, sort of watching myself go about my business. I'd been working seven days a week and I was stressed out — I felt like my body was pumping out adrenaline 24 hours a day, like I was permanently in danger and needing to run. By now, though, I'd had years of pretending I felt okay when

I didn't, so I buried what was going on and tried to push the anxiety as far down as I could. Surely if I didn't say what was going on out loud, then it wouldn't be real?

I didn't know what else to do other than keep going. I'd never had a mental breakdown so I didn't know that *that* was where I was headed — into Menty-B Land.

* * *

Before I go on, I need to talk about Antonio 'Bruno' Tomasel. Dad's dad, Nonno, the heart of our family. He was a warm, wonderful, fun and funny man, who never lost his thick Italian accent, love of hard work and sense of fun. Even though he died when I was five, I still have vivid memories. Nonno was well into his seventies when he got sick, but everyone says he looked more like 60. He had tanned skin from working outside his whole life, a tall muscular physique, and in my memories of him he's always smiling. His laughter lit up a whole room.

After Nonno and Nonna left their farm, in their sixties, they stayed super-active. They used to go walking all the time, worked in their garden six hours a day, and played bowls at the weekends. But before long, Nonno started complaining he couldn't walk as far anymore. He was limping and his coordination felt off. He ignored it until Nonna and Dad told him: 'Enough. Time to see the doctor.'

There were lots of tests, they took him to every specialist

they could think of, but no one could get to the bottom of why he was finding it hard to walk. Eventually, a year and a half after the problems first started, Nonno saw a local doctor he hadn't met before. After checking Nonno over and listening to what had been going on, he ushered my grandparents out to the waiting room and called my dad back into the little consulting room. No one in the family had noticed that Nonno's speech had changed, I guess because they saw him every day and the change was very gradual. But this doctor had picked up a very slight slur when Nonno spoke. It was the clue he needed.

'I think I know what's wrong with your dad,' the doctor said. 'I am not going to say what I think it is, but you need to take him to a neurologist as soon as possible.'

Dad drove Nonno to see a neurologist in Brisbane. He read the notes, heard what had been going on — and didn't hesitate. Looking Nonno in the eyes, he said: 'Bruno, I hate to tell you this, but you have motor neurone disease.'

It was a crushing diagnosis. Motor neurone disease is a degenerative neurological condition that affects the nerves and brain. It gets worse over time, and moving around, swallowing and breathing would become increasingly difficult for Nonno.

'Unfortunately, there is no cure,' said the neurologist.

'How long have I got?' asked Nonno.

'Eight months.'

No one expected such devastating news. Everyone in the family, including Nonno himself, thought he would carry on into his nineties — he was so fit and well and had so much love for life. Other than this horrible disease, everything else was in perfect working order.

Nonno went downhill really quickly after the diagnosis, losing the ability to walk and just wasting away in front of our eyes. Dad visited him every day, often twice a day. Nonno's speech was deteriorating, which was heartbreaking because he was a talker — always telling stories from the past and making sure us grandkids knew our Italian heritage. Now he was unintelligible. It was brutal for him because his mind was still sharp, and also brutal for the people around him.

When swallowing and breathing got really hard, he was taken to hospital in Brisbane. Dad slept in a chair next to him for four or five nights while the doctors tried to make him comfortable. At one point a doctor noted that Nonno still had some strength in his arms and suggested he might be staging a comeback. But a nurse who'd overheard took Dad aside and said: 'Don't listen to him — your dad is nearing the end. Take him home and make him comfortable. He doesn't want to be in here. Get him home so he can spend his final days as a family.'

Dad's always been grateful to that nurse, because it meant that Nonno was able to spend his last days on earth with the people he loved. Dad packed his things, drove him home, and carried him up the stairs in his arms like a baby. In less than six months, he'd gone from being a big, strong, muscly guy to a skeletal old man. Dad tucked Nonno into the bed he'd shared with Nonna for over 50 years. Everyone knew he didn't have much longer.

Next morning, Nonna rang Dad and his brothers and said 'You better come, your dad wants to see you.' Nonno couldn't talk anymore, but when Dad arrived he kept pointing to Nonna and back to Dad. It was clear he was asking Dad to take care of her when he was gone. Although Dad didn't want to believe this really was the end, he promised he would be there for Nonna. A few moments later, Nonno shut his eyes and drifted away. It was eight months to the day the specialist had made the diagnosis.

Our whole family was shocked, but Dad was devastated. Parents try to keep that sort of stuff from their kids, and I was only five or six, but I felt the impact of Dad's grief and it stayed with me. Of course I didn't realise at the time, but I would store away the trauma of Nonno's illness and death and it would come back to haunt me later in life.

At Nonna's funeral, I looked up at Dad and saw he was crying. That felt shocking to me — until then, I hadn't known dads could cry. I got used to it, though, because Dad cried a lot after Nonno died. He became hard to live with. He was pissed off that he'd lost his dad and pissed off that Nonno had missed out on his retirement. He'd worked so hard all his life that this just felt cruel. Dad spiralled into a deep depression for two years. He never got help. To deal with it, he threw himself into work, often not coming home off the farm till ten or eleven at night. Everyone around him was worried.

* * *

MENTY-B #1

Fast-forward to Brisbane, 2015. I should have been happy. I was co-hosting the weekend show at Nova, one of the biggest radio stations in Australia. I had lovely friends and a great social life. I had a nice flat in a townhouse I shared with Gawndy, and Mum and Dad visited me a lot. But I was stressed. I was working full-time in the street team from Monday to Friday and on weekends I was getting up at 4 a.m. for my breakfast show with Gawndy. But I'd made it — this was what I wanted! So I refused to listen to the little niggling signs that perhaps things weren't that great in my head.

'I'm okay, I'm okay,' I chanted silently, willing it to be true. But I wasn't okay. I was working too much. The stress was getting to me, and the pressure was building. Instead of pulling back a bit or talking to someone about maybe reducing my hours, I decided I would just work harder. I got obsessive. 'How can I take a day off? If I take time off they'll replace me.'

As per usual, fatalist thinking took hold of me. No matter how hard I tried, it was like my brain was working against me. There was a storm in my head, waves of negative thoughts pushing up against every corner of my mind. The fear and panic felt relentless.

Monday morning, 7 a.m., and I was getting ready for work. I looked in the mirror, pulled my hair back in a ponytail and splashed water on my face. 'Time to wake up, Bree.' I looked in the mirror again and — hold on, what's that? Something on my ear. What is that? Is it a freckle? *Shit*. It's a freckle! A freckle I've never noticed before. How could it have come up so quickly?

My heart started to race. Fuck, what if it was a skin cancer? It probably was a skin cancer, I told myself. I tried to push the thoughts to the back of my mind, but it was no use. The anxiety seed had been planted and 'I no longer had control over my thoughts. I have cancer and I'm going to die.'

Looking back, this was like an adult version of my first panic attack after the home invasion when I was a kid. I felt exactly the same as that day when I saw that mozzie bite on my hand and my brain told me it was a deadly spider bite. This time, it was a freckle making my brain spin out of control.

I went to work and tried to forget about the fact I was dying. When I was on-air I was okay, the thoughts were dulled. The minute I was off — wham, they were back. 'What about that freckle? It's probably growing right now and spreading. It's a full-blown melanoma and I'm screwed.' That voice in my head was getting louder and telling me with absolute certainty that this freckle was fatal. I was petrified; no one wants to die at 26. I had my whole life ahead of me. Why me?

I went to the doctor, who took one look and told me it was a normal freckle and nothing to be worried about. But because I was freaking out she referred me to a skin specialist 'just to be sure'.

Just to be sure. Just to be sure? Just to be sure!!! Huh, I knew it — I *knew* this was serious.

Writing this now, I realise how crazy I sound. But anyone in the grip of a breakdown or crippling anxiety will understand the tricks your brain can play on you. At this point my brain was the world's best magician. At night I lay awake in bed, carefully listening to every part of my body to feel the cancer spreading. An ache here, a tingle there. All proof, of course, that the cancer was aggressive. I could almost feel the sickness moving through me. Sleep became impossible. I was existing on a couple of hours each night. Night terrors struck. A black shadowy figure would float into my room and hover over me. It would pick me up and drag me down the hallway of the townhouse, throwing me against the walls and onto the floor. When I woke, screaming, I was drenched in sweat and felt like I was having a heart attack.

But I kept going to work — getting up and showering each day, putting on my make-up and plastering a fake smile on my dial to get me through. On the inside I felt like a zombie. The freckle was on my mind constantly. 'Bree, are you sure you're okay?' people at work would ask. 'Yeah, I'm okay,' I would lie.

During the day I was on auto-pilot, but when I got home everything fell apart. I spent hours lying on my bed, staring up at the ceiling, imagining my death. I stopped eating. I ignored friends' messages and phone calls. And I was a slave to Google, desperately searching for evidence to support my crazy belief that I was a goner. 'Melanoma symptoms' 'How long to die from first noticing freckle?' 'Is melanoma painful?' 'How to accept cancer'.

I now know I was in the grips of a mental breakdown caused by health anxiety which at its core, is a fear of death. I believe whole-heartedly my mental health problems are directly linked to what happened to me when I was nine. When those men had us trapped in Nan's house, knife at my throat, I believed so deeply I was going to die and I have never been able to fully shake that feeling. The trauma changed my brain, and took away my ability to work through stress and worries in a healthy way. Instead, when I reach that point I go straight to pure terror, and right back to that day where all I can think is 'I'm going to die, I'm going to die.' Nonno's illness and death only fuelled my fear of death. Health anxiety is an actual disorder where someone worries excessively that they are, or will become, seriously ill. It's a long-term condition that can fluctuate in severity. 'It may increase with age or during times of stress,' says the internet. Ah, times of stress. That was the clincher.

Of course, at the time I didn't think I was going crazy because of health anxiety. I thought I was going crazy BECAUSE I WAS DYING. And I became so consumed by my fears that I actually started having physical symptoms. There were pains in my arms and my feet, and my hands were constantly shaking. A quick google confirmed my fears: I had multiple sclerosis, or, even worse, motor neurone disease like Nonno. It had finally come to get me.

About a week in to this, I realised I was in real shit and needed help.

'Mum, I'm falling apart.'

'I'm coming, Brianna. Hang on till I get there.'

Mumma Di dropped everything and got straight in her car, because that's the sort of goddess mother she is. She turned up to find me in a complete state. My mind had trapped me in a whirlwind of shit. I showed her the cancerous freckle and begged her to help me find proper medical assistance. 'I need a CAT scan,' I said, earnestly. 'That's the only way we'll be able to see how far it's spread.'

Mum could see I'd lost the plot entirely, but she went along with it. She was trying to work out the best way to deal with me. While she knew I wasn't dying, she could see I was having some kind of breakdown, and she hoped that a scan would prove to me my body wasn't riddled with cancer. I don't know how she managed to get a doctor on board, but the next day she took me to a radiology place in Brisbane, where I prepared for my CAT scan which would tell me how long I had left. I was terrified.

Afterwards, the doctor sat me and Mum down in his office to deliver the results. I held on to Mum's hand and braced myself for the news.

'There is nothing on the scan that is of concern, but I believe you are mentally unwell and you need some help,' said the doctor.

I pretended I understood, but I still wasn't convinced. That scanner machine could have been broken, right? Those machines aren't perfect, we all know that. But it did give me the jolt I needed to understand that it was my mind that was part of the problem. I went back to my GP, who was shocked at the sight of me. It had only been a few weeks since my first visit, but I hadn't really slept or eaten in that time. I'd lost about 5 kg. My eyes were glazed over and my hands were shaking. I looked like I'd gone twelve rounds with Mike Tyson.

The GP prescribed an anti-anxiety drug, diazepam, to take the edge off and allow me to get some sleep. 'Your body needs rest.' She was right; I was exhausted. Mum drove me home and I took the pill and climbed into bed. That lovely little pill washed over me, my muscles relaxed, my brain calmed down and, finally, I slept. Blessed fucking relief.

Mum stayed with me for a week, sleeping with me in my bed at night to help keep me safe from my wild animal of a mind. Once again, I was that little girl being kept safe by Mum after the knife incident. She fed me, dropped me off at work each day, and was there at the end of my shift waiting to take me home. An absolute angel. And once I started getting some sleep, helped by the little white pill I would pop each night to help me drift off, things slowly started to improve. I got stronger and managed to accept that I'd escaped death — this time. I felt changed, though. I went into myself. I didn't see friends, I ignored messages, I turned down invites. I existed solely to work. I felt broken and exhausted, scared by what happened and afraid it could happen again.

For the next few months, it felt like my brain was at war with itself. The rational part was constantly fighting with the hypothetical part, the side that focused and obsessed on the what-ifs and the endless fucking negativity. I knew I had to pull myself out of it, and that the only person who could do that was me. It was exhausting, but over time I got better. But the emotional bruises were there for a long time, as was the fear that it would happen again.

Pride

I hated 2017. It was the year Australians were able to vote on same-sex marriage. The vote was voluntary and the results non-binding, so in lots of ways it meant nothing. But it also meant everything.

I was living proof that stigma, shame and intolerance still existed. I held a girl's hand in public once, only to have some prick slow down in his car, lean his head out the window and shout 'DYKES!' I never held anyone's hand that way again. I was so riddled with fear and shame that I was still hiding my true self from my dad, and I didn't have the balls to come out at work, either. It's no surprise, I guess, that this vote felt personal. And to me and my queer friends, the vote represented much more than whether we could marry the person we loved. It was about equality. The results would show us how other people felt about us. It would show how far, or not far, society had come.

And it would give a real indication of the level of intolerance and bigotry in Australia. This vote magnified the feelings I was having every day — the fear of being judged or excluded because of who I was.

I'd never felt so personally connected to politics before, and I know most of my queer friends felt the same. It was like the public was being asked if we were deserving of equal rights, equal status. And if the answer was no, what did that mean? That we were lesser people? That we didn't deserve the same as heterosexual people?

The vote had everyone talking. It was forcing conversations to happen, and that heightened the shame that had settled just beneath my surface. There were campaigns on the TV and radio both for and against gay marriage, all of it feeling very personal. I couldn't get away from it and I felt exposed. As the vote got closer, it seemed like it was all people talked about. Friend groups were divided, families were arguing, and tension was running high. Even though a yes result was expected, based on early polls, I felt a sense of dread. It's a very weird feeling to be the subject of a national vote which, at its heart, was about equality.

Unsurprisingly, the Catholic church opposed same-sex marriage. And I had a pretty good idea what Dad's views would be. I hadn't planned to talk to him about it, because I was afraid of what he might say, but when he and Mum came to stay with me one weekend I couldn't help myself. We were watching TV and one of those nasty ads had come on with some old loser telling people that marriage was sacred and should be reserved for men and women.

'Dad, are you going to vote for same-sex marriage or against?' I asked. I felt like crying. I didn't want to hear the answer, so why the fuck did I ask?

Dad looked at me and took a breath. In that instant I felt pretty convinced that he knew about me and was choosing not to address it. 'Well, my beliefs are that marriage should be between a man and a woman. So based on that, I suppose I'll be voting no.'

Fucking hell. Something in me unleashed. 'But why should your religious beliefs impact equal human rights? Is this about religion? Or is it about everyone — no matter their sexuality — being able to do the same as other people, and having the same rights around that?'

There was no stopping me.

'That's what this is about, Dad. It's not about religious beliefs or what you were told growing up — it's about equal human rights. Why should one human being have different rights to another human being based on who they love?'

He was quiet for a bit, and I know he could see how passionately I believed in what I was saying. Finally, he reluctantly said: 'Well, I guess, based on that argument I should probably vote yes.'

I went into my bedroom and burst into tears. It was the closest I'd got to coming out to Dad and I was a mess.

I didn't learn from my mistakes, though. A few days later I was getting my nails done with my sister Amber and stupidly asked how *she* was going to vote. I had a firm suspicion she and Dad shared similar views, so I should have left the topic alone. But I was obsessed with this vote and obsessed with working out which way people were going.

'I don't mind if they have the same rights, but it shouldn't be called marriage because it's not marriage, it's something else,' Amber said. I have no idea if she knew I was queer, but this felt like the biggest slap in the face. She might as well have told me she thought I was a lesser person than she was.

I said nothing, but what I wish I'd said was, 'Why is it not the same?' I wanted to scream and shout and cry. But I didn't. I turned my head, stared at the wall and blinked away the tears that were threatening. It only strengthened my resolve not to tell her the truth about me. I was pretty sure I would never come out to Dad and Amber.

* * *

At work, I was learning the thing that all radio hosts learn: the more I was myself on-air, the better I was at my job. The more I shared from my life, the better the reaction I got from listeners, guests and colleagues. It wasn't just okay to be myself on air — it was actually essential. But there was a problem. I wasn't being 100% authentic because there was a big part of me that was off-limits. While Gawndy and I went through lots of life stages together and he knew everything about me, we both knew that my relationship stories weren't for the radio. He was super-open about his girlfriends and dating and eventually he got married, which gave us lots of stuff to talk about on-air. He was amazing at using his relationship for content. I couldn't do that. And it made me sad. I wanted to be like Gawndy, I wanted to be free to talk about every part of my life.

At first, it was my call to keep it under wraps. I wasn't ready. But after we moved our show to Sea FM on the Central Coast, it was playing on my mind so I spoke to one of my bosses at work. I said, 'I'm wondering if it might be time to be honest about my sexuality . . . what do you think?' This person, who I won't name, wasn't being deliberately horrible and I like to think they had my best interests at heart, but they said: 'This is a small town. You need to think about your audience and cater to them. Maybe it's not the right time . . . you don't want to harm your career, either.'

'Yeah, yeah, cool, no problem,' I lied.

I was devastated. It had taken heaps of courage to go to them for their opinion and I felt totally shot down. It confirmed my fears that my true self wasn't right for radio, that I'd never be accepted for who I am. It made me feel like my sexuality meant people would never truly like me.

I continued to lean heavily on my family and friends for content instead. Thank god for Mum, she'd always been such a huge character and was so good-hearted about letting me use her for radio. She provided me with so much to talk about that it wasn't like I was struggling to come up with stories. It was just that I wished I was considered 'normal'. I wished I could share the same sorts of dating and domestic stories my heterosexual co-host shared. It didn't seem fair.

And with the looming marriage-equality vote I was feeling a growing sense of responsibility. I had a platform, which is such a huge privilege, and I knew I could use it. I should have been proud of who I was and using my voice to show people that being gay is okay. That people like me should be able to marry whoever they want and that the world would continue to spin and nothing terrible would happen. I wanted to shout it from the rooftops, but I was a massive fucking scaredy-cat. Scared of my dad's reaction, my sister's, and worried too it might affect my employment, my popularity and my future job prospects.

At one point, we had local MP Lucy Wicks on the show. She'd gained lots of media attention because she'd been so outspoken about her opposition to marriage equality. While I wasn't brave enough to come out on-air, I did have the guts to take on this homophobic town crier — I'd had enough of bullshit like hers. Over ten minutes (a bloody long interview for radio), I made it my mission to tell her exactly how damaging this vote and views like hers were for the queer community.

My blood was boiling but I was calm and clear as I tore apart the tiny arguments she presented. She had nothing to offer other than a belief that Australians deserved a say on whether people like me deserved the same rights as people like her. I felt like I had the responsibility of my entire community on my shoulders and I simply had to do this. I've never felt so committed to nailing an interview.

PRIDE

I asked Lucy to explain why she felt it was okay that everyone in Australia should get to vote on whether queer people deserved the same rights as everyone else. I asked her if she'd considered the mental health effects of this vote on young gay people. I made it crystal-clear how deeply wrong I believed the whole thing was — and in the end, I felt like I had her up against the ropes. She was flailing and truly had nothing to back up her anti-equality stance. This is one of the interviews I'm most proud of from my entire career, and I like to think it might have encouraged some listeners to think twice before they voted. Most importantly, I wanted people from the queer community to hear my voice and know they had support out there.

When I left the studio that day, I was amazed to find a bunch of people waiting to see me in reception. I was terrified it might be homophobic psychos come to run me out of town. But it was the opposite — listeners had driven to the Sea FM office to thank me for taking Lucy Wicks on and for standing up for the queer community. It's the first and only time that people have turned up like that, and it's something I'll never forget.

* * *

In the end, over 60% of Australians voted in support of same-sex marriage and the law was changed in December 2017. Halle-fucken-lujah, same-sex marriage was finally legal. Better late than never, Aussie. People took to the streets to celebrate, pride flags flying, you know the drill. I didn't go. Don't get me wrong: I was happy with the result and I'm sure I would've joined in the celebrations if I'd lived somewhere like Melbourne or Sydney. But I was on the Central Coast, in a sleepy little place, and there was no sign of street parties breaking out there. And I felt exhausted. The vote had dominated my thoughts for months and had been a big part of my work life too, with conversations and debate over the topic happening most days on-air. I felt surprisingly flat; lots of my gay friends felt the same.

And for some reason, I couldn't shake off my anger. It was 2017, not 1917 — yet the government had spent some crazy amount like $22 million on this vote that wasn't even binding. They already had the statistics and data long before the votes were counted, and those showed that the majority of Australians supported same-sex marriage. So why did they need a non-binding vote? All that did was give the homophobes and bigots permission to spout their shit. It reminded every queer person in Australia that almost half the people around them didn't like them, didn't support them, and didn't care about their equality. It pissed me off — why should Damian down the road be given a say over who I should or shouldn't be allowed to marry? He can marry whoever the hell he wants, so why can't I?

Even though we got the yes result, I came out of that time feeling like the world was more divided than ever. Instead of encouraging me to come out, or feel proud of who I was, it forced me back even further into my shell. On one level I was sure Dad had worked out I was gay, yet his unwillingness to tell me it was okay was causing me real pain. I still couldn't work out if he was completely blind to what was in front of him or if he was deliberately choosing not to front up to it because it felt unacceptable. I continued to take my girlfriends back to Stanthorpe, but they were referred to as 'Brianna's friend'. Separate beds would be made up and everyone was in on the charade. Why? I still don't understand why my family, me included, carried on like this for so long.

One Christmas I finally cracked. Mum found me sobbing in my room. 'What's wrong, Brianna?' she asked, even though she knew exactly what was wrong. Amber and Aden's partners were there with the family, sitting at the table, eating, drinking, laughing and being included. Yet my partner wasn't there.

'I'm so sick of this,' I told her. 'I'm sick of missing out. I'm sick of being the only one who isn't treated normally. I hate this. I am sick of having to think about how everyone else is feeling and making sure no one feels uncomfortable.' Mum was desperate to tell Dad, because she could see this secret had grown into a giant monster of a problem. But she'd made her promise and she wasn't about to break it.

* * *

Picture this: It's 2018. I'm 29 years old and I'm at the premiere of a movie called *Love, Simon*. It's a sweet little film about a high-school kid coming to terms with being gay. Simon is like me: he's nervous about telling his parents who he really is. But finally, brave little Simon plucks up the courage to tell them. His mum is lovely and supportive, but his dad takes a little longer to process the news. After a few days, though, his dad comes to him, hugs him and says he will always love him.

This hits me right in the guts and I momentarily forget it's a movie and not real. I can't believe that this kid is seventeen and has the balls to talk to his dad and face whatever comes, yet here I am, nearly 30 and still too fucking scared.

'That's it,' I tell myself. 'I'm going to tell him.' I walk out of that cinema more determined than ever. I've had enough of the secrecy and I'm sick of feeling shit about myself. I grab my phone and call Dad.

'Hi, Dad.' I can't believe I'm finally about to do it.

'Hello Pumpkin, how are you? What've you been up to?'

I tell him I've been at the movies. I tell him how work's going and what my weekend plans are. I tell him every single fucking thing EXCEPT THE ONE THING I HAVE CALLED TO TELL HIM. We chat for 45 minutes. And I can't do it. I can't say the words I've been wanting to say for almost ten years.

I hate myself. I know I am the problem here. Why have I let this happen? After saying goodbye to Dad, I sit in the car in the driveway of my house and cry. 'What's wrong with me? Why can't I do it?' I have no idea. But this secret has grown so big and out of control it feels like it was never, ever going to be talked about. It feels like a mountain that is just too steep to climb.

Gay panic

I don't want you for a moment to think it sucks to be queer. Listen to me: it *does not suck!* It's actually completely fabulous and even though it's taken me a while to be comfortable in my own skin, I wouldn't change who I am for anything. Because I LOVE being queer. I could give you so many reasons why it's awesome, but the best thing is that you get immediate access to a really wonderful club. And this is a fact: the global queer club is filled with some of the best people on earth. If there are any boring gays, bring them to me because I've yet to meet one. Admit it: the gay people you know are creative, funny and fun. We're loyal and kind and non-judgemental. We have the best parties and the best friends and we are, well, you know, fucking *great!*

The friendships in this club are tight. We are all united by shared experiences. Every single one of us has gone through something to work out who we are and where we fit in. Of course, some people have easier rides than others in terms of coming out and living freely. Some of us are out and proud and loved by everyone that matters to them. Others are still firmly in the closet with no plans to step out, and lots more are somewhere in between. It doesn't matter, really — the thing that bonds us is that we all get it. There's a concept in the queer community we call our 'chosen family'. In the gay world, the phrase 'You can choose your friends but you can't choose your family' doesn't apply. We can and we do, and for our chosen families we pick the best people around. Or sometimes they pick us. We might not be biologically related, but the friends in our chosen family are connected through unconditional love. When someone gets rejected or disowned by their real family, the chosen family steps in. We pick up the pieces and fill the gap, essentially providing the love and support that's been withheld simply because of who the person is. Our chosen family never judges and always allows people the space to be completely themselves.

But I wish someone had told 25-year-old me that being queer was great and that being queer was nothing to be ashamed of. I wish someone had sat me down and told me that being queer was what made me special. That it made me creative, different and unique. It has given me an empathy and compassion for others that I don't think I would have had otherwise. I wish someone had told me that once you start living authentically, everything will fall into place. Living truthfully — especially if it's taken some time to get there — brings such immense joy.

GAY PANIC

It brings relief and joy and a determination to grab life by the fucking horns and *live* it.

That's the good stuff, and I try to focus on that when I have a hard day. What I find exhausting, though, is the daily decision-making about who I come out to. It's a myth that gay people come out just once in their lives: a big, fabulous reveal and they live happily ever after. Gay people have to come out *all* the time, often several times a day. What I mean by that is we are constantly faced with micro-moments where we must decide whether to reveal our sexuality. I might be on the phone to an insurance company and the person will ask for my partner's details. Or I'll meet someone new at the gym or in a cafe and they'll ask if I have a boyfriend. A new person might start at work and I can't help but wonder when I should tell them. When will the inevitable reveal occur?

* * *

Life can feel like one great big heteronormative assumption, because most people — whether they're aware they're doing it or not — just assume everyone is straight. So every time someone wrongly assumes my partner is a man, I have to decide: do I bother to correct them? Do I tell them my partner is a woman? And before I can make that decision, I have to make a lightning-quick calculation about the person in front or me or at the other end of the phone. Because the thing I've learned is you don't *know* how people are going to take it. You don't *know* who you can talk openly with. You don't know their belief systems or prejudices. So I have to take this person in and try to work out where they sit on the homophobe scale. Does this person seem old-fashioned? Could they be religious? Will they judge me? And that means there's a risk element every time I decide to be honest about who I am. I am not a naturally guarded sort of person — I want to be open and honest. But this little seed of fear means I constantly have my guard up as a self-protection measure.

Straight privilege is everywhere. It is the unearned and often unconscious benefits that heterosexual people get in society and gay people don't. I could list a million ways in which straight privilege plays out, but here are a few examples:

- Straight people's identities aren't determined by their sexuality.
- People don't assume a straight person knows every other straight person just because they're straight.
- Straight people aren't forced to confront, explain or consider their sexuality on a daily basis.
- Straight people don't have to seek out representation in TV, books and movies.
- Straight people don't have to worry about friends, family or co-workers finding out about their sexual orientation and it having negative consequences.
- Straight people can hold their loved one's hand in public without the fear of being abused.

- Straight people's sexual orientation isn't used as a slur: 'That's so *gay*.'
- People don't assume straight people are attracted to and want to have sex with every member of the opposite sex they meet.
- Straight people don't face violence or fear for their safety because of their sexuality.

Maybe I don't look the way people think lesbians should look, because people are always assuming I'm straight. And sometimes I can't be bothered correcting them. Why should I have to reveal my sexuality every bloody day? Heterosexual people don't have to, do they? They just live their lives with the wonderful privilege of being 'normal'.

Most of the time though, I tell the truth. I correct people when they ask about my boyfriend or husband and I ignore the little change in energy when I tell someone my partner's name. Mostly it's not a big deal, people are lovely and my day continues on. Other times, though, I hear the surprise in their voice. Or I see a look of distaste pass over their face. I register that little moment of judgement. And I know that this person now thinks less of me than they did a couple of seconds earlier.

I'd love to say that doesn't hurt. But it does. It really fucking hurts because I still can't quite believe I live in a world where I am outside what's considered normal. I have this internal push and pull: I want to be out and proud, but the little things add up and I can't quite escape my shame and embarrassment.

There's also an inner battle with myself where I'm thinking 'Am I nervous to tell this person because I'm ashamed? Is that why I'm not saying it?'

There are other situations, too, that I have grown to dread. Checking into hotels with my partner Sophia can be awkward. Receptionists assume we're friends, or sisters, so we'll be given a room with twin beds. Then we have the embarrassing task of asking to be moved to a room with a double bed, like a pair of sexual deviants. Except we're not sexual deviants, we're just a couple who would like to share a bed. Sometimes we don't bother with the faff. Travelling at all as a gay person can make you feel vulnerable. If we want to go overseas, we always check the safety ratings for gay travellers. We have to weigh up if a country is safe for us to be together as a couple.

So yes, this stuff is hard and tiring and I hate it. But going through it together with the people in our chosen family makes it bearable. We laugh about it, we share the ridiculous things that happen to us, and we seek out the people who we can be ourselves with. I realise how lucky I am to have a real family who loves me for who I am, even if it did take a while to get there. I know how much worse other people have it and my heart breaks for them. And this is where our chosen families are so important. Sophia and I have a very close friend who we consider our brother. His actual family has been less than ideal when it comes to accepting his sexuality, and I've seen how it's torn him apart. You can be as staunch as you like, but the knowledge that your family can only accept part of you causes such damage. Our friend went home

GAY PANIC

recently wearing fabulous colourful beads around his neck, only for his mum to hiss 'You'd better take those off before your father sees them — you know it will make him uncomfortable.'

It's that shit, that knowledge your own family — the people who are supposed to love you no matter what — can't embrace you for who you are that tears away at you piece by piece. Eventually it all comes to a head. You have to do something about it or you will implode. The damage caused to someone whose family can't love them unconditionally is so deep and so heavy it breaks my heart. But the joy, oh man, the *joy* that queer people have when they're finally able to be themselves and lead the lives they were destined to live — well, that's a magical thing to be part of. It's the thing that straight people get automatically — not that I'm bitter or anything; just a wee bit jealous.

But for all the shit we queer people have to go through, the world we inhabit is special. It's vibrant and covered in glitter, and I am grateful to be a part of it.

✳ ✳ ✳

Maybe I'm approachable, I don't know, but people often seem to come to me for gay guidance. I'm like Gay Gandalf, the wise old wizard of the gays if you will. I don't know why people think I'm the holder of all homosexual knowledge, but I do my best to assist. 'Thou shalt take it up the rear!'

I joke, but if someone is curious about their sexuality, it's often me they'll talk to. It's often me they'll share their gay panic with. 'Calm your farm,' I tell them. 'I know this might seem like the biggest deal in the world, but it really isn't. Take your time, have fun, and you'll figure it out.'

People are always very curious about sex between girls. One of the most common queries is people wanting to know what actually constitutes lesbian sex. 'Is it this? Or is it that?' they ask. My answer? I don't bloody know! Sex is what you want it to be. What floats one person's boat might not float another's. My sex might not be your sex. You get the picture. But if you really want to know, in my experience girl-on-girl equals more orgasms, simple as that. The reason being that women have an inbuilt GPS system. No need to ask for directions; we all know exactly how to get to the destination without any wrong turns leading us off-track or up a dirt road.

Sometimes, people want support if they've identified certain unfamiliar feelings. They want to know that what they're feeling is okay, or they just need a little push from someone saying, 'It's fine, go figure yourself out.' Or sometimes someone might have had an experience with someone of the same sex and they're full of doubt, shame and loathing, wondering what it all means. 'Does this mean I'm gay?' they'll ask.

My answer: you don't need to work out if you're gay or not. IT. DOES. NOT. MATTER. Don't waste your time trying to figure out how to label yourself. Just be you. A girl could have a full-on relationship with another girl and turn around afterwards and say, 'Actually, I think it was just that woman I was attracted to.'

That's fine! There are no rules. If you want to hook up with girls one week and boys the next, just bloody go for it. You do *you*.

Society is fixated on finding labels for everyone. If I had a dollar for every time someone asked if I was gay, straight or bi, I'd be a rich woman. For me, sexuality is about doing and trusting a feeling and not being governed by what other people are going to think or having to put a label on yourself. I would not change who I am. And the people who love me wouldn't change who I am. Mum tells me every single day how much she loves me *as I am*. She says: 'I know there are parts of your life that are really hard, but you wouldn't be who you are without those.'

And she's right. There is a reason for every single part of me. And my sexuality is something I value about myself now. My experiences growing up have given me an empathy and an emotional intelligence I would not have had otherwise. I am a deeper, more compassionate and understanding person because of that.

A leap of faith

Back in 2015 when we were still at Nova in Brisbane, Gawndy and I were getting restless. We loved our little weekend show, but we were ambitious and we had big dreams.

We had good ratings, we were making content that listeners seemed to love and the bosses were happy, so we knew our show was good enough to go full-time. The problem was, though, there were no openings at Nova so we needed to look for opportunities further afield than Brisbane. Gawndy and I sent off demo tapes to pretty much every big station in the country. And over the course of a few weeks we got many, many 'no thank yous' until, finally, a more positive email arrived from someone at 101.3 Sea FM — a provincial radio station on the Central Coast, about an hour north of Sydney.

'Exciting!' you might think. Well, yes, it was exciting for

A LEAP OF FAITH

Gawndy but not so exciting for me. Sea FM offered Gawndy a role but were not interested in taking me with him. WTF? We were a double-act, we'd been building it up for three years, and we'd approached them as a package deal; we couldn't go out on our own! Except that deep down we both knew Gawndy had to accept the job. 'You gotta take it,' I told him. My bruised ego and I did our best to be happy for Gawndy as we waved him off from Nova and on to the next big thing.

As it turned out, Gawndy got wind that another presenter at Sea FM was leaving. There could be a position coming available. He'd always had an uncanny ability to find out what was going on in any workplace, so it was no surprise when one of the Sea FM hosts announced her resignation soon afterwards. 'This has your name on it, Bree,' he said. Gawndy told the bosses that this was the perfect opportunity to hire me. They weren't convinced, though, and made him audition with a whole bunch of other potential hosts. He didn't feel he had great chemistry with any of them, so went in to bat again for me and again asked, 'What about Bree?'

'She's an unknown, she doesn't have full-time radio experience, she's a risk,' they told him.

'I'm telling you, she'll do a great job,' he said.

Back and forwards, back and forwards . . . till eventually they gave in to Gawndy and agreed to audition me. But it wasn't until I said I would edit and cut videos as part of my role that they finally agreed to take me on. Thank god for all those years I'd spent on YouTube teaching myself to edit videos. Usually this is a separate job to the radio announcer role, but by getting me doing it they could save on an entire salary. And it was this that got the bosses across the line: two jobs for the price of one. Tight-arses.

Not that I cared — I was bloody stoked! This was the moment when I knew the years of hard work and grind had finally paid off. Gawndy and I had our own full-time breakfast show: The Bree and Gawndy Show; we'd bloody done it! This was huge for my career. I was 27 and had achieved my dream of working full-time as a radio announcer. The awkward little bogan from Queensland could barely wipe the smile off her face as she packed up her Brisbane life for a new one on the Central Coast.

* * *

Of course, day one rolled around and I was absolutely shitting my pants. What if it was a flop? What if everyone hated me? Thank god I had Gawndy next to me to help keep my anxiety in check. He was not only a workmate but also a wonderful friend, and it felt like we'd grown up together during our time at Nova. We had each other's backs and together we made it our mission to create a great experience for our listeners. And we did pretty well, climbing to the number-one spot after not very long and staying there for the next couple of years.

A year in, we were asked to do a national Saturday breakfast show as well as our weekday gig. The show was aired on every

A LEAP OF FAITH

regional station in Australia. It meant we were working six days a week, but I didn't care because I was doing what I loved. And let's face it, I might as well have been working because I didn't have much else to do. I was a Nigel No-Mates with zero social life in a town where I knew no one. It turns out it's quite hard making friends when you're an adult.

Maybe this was why I started mucking around on Instagram and Facebook. I got so bored sitting at home at night that I'd make little videos of me doing stupid shit, mainly to entertain myself. I didn't really expect anything much when I posted these little bits and bobs, but weirdly, people seemed to like them. They weren't groundbreakingly funny or clever or anything, it was just me being me — telling dumb jokes, acting like an idiot, putting together little comedy skits and sharing stories about the weird shit that happened to me each day. But things really took off when I roped Mum into these videos. People fucking LOVED her.

The brilliance of Mumma Di was not news to me; she's always been the greatest person I know. She's good in all the ways a mum is meant to be, y'know? Supportive, loving, always there for us, makes the dinner, does the washing, never complains, that kind of thing. But then there's this other side to her that is simply hysterical. Intentionally or, more often than not, unintentionally, Mum can make me piss myself laughing more than anyone else. She is so fun to be around because her reactions are so freaking amazing. People ask me if she only screams 'Oh, Brianna!' when I've got my phone out filming, but I can assure you she's been saying that since the day I was bloody born. She was my first audience as an attention-seeking kid, always laughing as I danced around showing off at the most inappropriate moments, generously giving me what I craved. And she's never stopped, really. Even when she thinks my dirty jokes have gone too far, there's no mistaking the little smirk she's trying desperately to hide. Our conversations go something like this:

'Hey Mum, what do lesbians do when they're on their period?'

'What, Brianna?'

'They fingerpaint.'

'Oh, Brianna!'

She's a great crowd. And I can push the boundaries with Mum. She forgave me when I shared her phone number to hundreds of thousands of people on social media, telling them to get in touch with her on her birthday. Not only did she receive birthday messages and phone calls in their thousands, she was lucky enough to get a few nudes, too. She couldn't understand how so many people had her number and why they were messaging her and calling her. I'll admit, it took her a while to see the funny side when she found out I was to blame. Another time, I had a photo of her face turned into a cartoon and printed onto a thousand T-shirts which I sold on Instagram. They were a hit, selling out in less than a week! Mum pretends she hates this stuff but, because I know her so well, I have total confidence that she actually bloody loves it. And Mum herself has told me

A LEAP OF FAITH

that involving her in this stuff makes her feel special and seen. So often women can feel invisible as they get older, so it's my mission to make sure it's the complete opposite for Mumma Di. She deserves all the attention I can drum up.

Then there was this: a notification popped up on my Instagram telling me Channing Tatum had started following me. It's obviously not real, I thought; it must be some weird fake celebrity page. But I clicked on the link and it took me to Channing Tatum's official profile with the all-important blue tick. THE Channing Tatum, aka Magic Mike, the very, very famous Hollywood movie star with 12 million followers at the time. How the hell did he find me on Instagram? Little old me! I was still not entirely convinced it wasn't some sort of hoax, so I decided to message him.

'Hey Channing, cheers for the follow.'

He messaged me right back. 'You're fucking hilarious, I love the stuff with you and your mom.'

OH MY GOD. Channing Tatum watched my vids and thought I was funny! And he likes Mumma Di! This was too much. I messaged him back and we chatted for a while, hereby marking the beginning of my Channing Tatum Obsession Era. A few years later, as part of a radio stunt, I decided to meet my new bestie face-to-face. I didn't know how I'd pull it off, but I set out to Los Angeles to track him down. He liked me, remember — I was sure he'd agree to hang out and be on our radio show. And who knows, maybe after that we could be real best friends. Or, like, get married or something. I dunno. Even a *Magic Mike* lappie to Ginuwine's 'Pony' would have been a solid compromise.

The mission failed miserably. I flew into LA only to discover Channing wasn't even in the country. A year later, however, I did get the chance to interview him over Zoom and was stoked that he remembered me. 'How's your mom?' he asked. By this point I was getting the impression that he only had eyes for Mumma Di. She, of course, was delighted by this and for Christmas she gave me a life-sized Channing Tatum cardboard cut-out.

※ ※ ※

To my astonishment, during that first year of posting on social media my following went from a few thousand to a few *hundred thousand*. I had people from all over the world messaging and liking and sharing, and it would be a lie to say I was chill about it. It was awesome! Such a really cool feeling knowing that people were getting something out of the content I was creating. I was making them laugh, and that was like a drug to me. So I kept doing what I was doing. My formula was always the same: if I thought something was funny, I'd pop it on the 'gram and see how it went. And even though I've got a pretty good idea about the kind of stuff that makes people smile, I'm still surprised when things do well.

While I was living on the Central Coast in Australia, I didn't realise it but a guy in New Zealand called Dean Buchanan had started following me. He was then Group Content Director

A LEAP OF FAITH

Entertainment at NZME in New Zealand — i.e. the Big Radio Boss — and he'd somehow stumbled across my socials. He'd also started listening to my radio show. Dean had worked in broadcasting in Australia for years and knew the radio industry there well. He later told me he thought I was being overlooked and he couldn't understand why I hadn't been picked up by a bigger station. Sea FM was a small provincial network and Dean believed I was ready for more. He said I seemed original and he liked that I had my own style.

When ZM hosts Jase Hawkins (you know, Labby, the guy from B105 who inspired me all those years ago) and Polly 'PJ' Harding were poached from NZME by an Australian radio station, it was up to Dean to find new talent to fill their roles — and he immediately thought of me. He decided he wanted this random Aussie that no one in New Zealand had ever heard of to take over the afternoon drive show. The other Big Bosses must have thought he was crazy. I was a risk, there's no two ways about it. But somehow he managed to convince them that I was worth approaching. I'll always be grateful to Dean for that. He jokes that the one thing he's good at in life is spotting talent, but he's also the first man I ever worked for who would tell me when he thought I'd done something well. He championed me from the get-go, which is something I'll never forget.

Dean asked his former colleague Craig Bruce, a bigwig in Aussie radio, to give me a call to sound me out. I still remember the moment that call came through. I was walking to my car after our show when an unknown number popped up. Craig introduced himself and cut to the chase pretty quickly, asking if I might be interested in discussing a radio opportunity in New Zealand.

'New Zealand? What the hell?'

I was really confused. I suppose it was flattering that someone had taken notice of me, but I couldn't work out how anyone in *New Zealand* would have been aware of my existence — and why on earth they thought I was the right person for their job. The whole thing was a giant 'HUH?'

'Um, okay, yeah, I could talk to someone I guess,' I said. 'Thanks.'

Ross Flahive, my now-boss at ZM, called me later that day to explain the role and answer any questions I had. Unlike the little station I was at then, he told me ZM was a much bigger station that broadcast right across New Zealand. He wanted me to host the afternoon show from 3 to 7 p.m. on weekdays and said that finding me a co-host would be the next step. I listened politely and made the right noises, but I knew I couldn't move to New Zealand. I'd only visited a few times and while it was nice for a holiday, I didn't know anyone there and my whole life was in Australia. Besides, I'd worked so hard to get where I was in the Aussie radio market, I would have to be crazy to walk away from all that.

'I'll think about it,' I lied.

A few days later, the Big Boss, Dean, called me to see where I was at with the offer. I told him that while I was flattered and grateful to be approached, I wasn't interested in the job. I kept saying 'No thanks.' But they kept coming back. Emails, calls, texts . . . those Kiwis were persistent! Ross always reminds me that he's never chased a girl as hard as he had to chase me.

At the same time, I was having a frustrating time with renewing my contract at Sea FM. My boss wanted me to commit to another three years, but I was pissed off because I'd found out that Gawndy was being paid significantly more than me. I understood why there had been the pay discrepancy when they first hired me — I was less experienced than him so it made sense that I'd get paid less. But two years down the track I felt I deserved the same as my co-host. We worked the same hours, we'd built the show up together, we were rating really well, and together we were making great content. I couldn't understand why I was paid less. Was it because I was a woman?

The bosses denied that my gender had anything to do with it and said our salaries were based on our experience. They offered me a small pay increase, but it still didn't mean I would be paid equally and I was still pissed off.

Gawndy knew about the ZM offer and was trying hard to convince me not to take it. He believed in our show and told me that if I hung on in there, we were bound to get picked up by a bigger station soon. But I was still being bombarded by these bloody New Zealanders from ZM! They wouldn't give up, and discussions about the role went on for weeks and weeks. I was also being pressured to hurry up and renew that Sea FM contract. I was feeling the pressure from all sides. Not good for my anxiety levels.

Finally, with one of my bosses standing over me, I felt I had no choice but to re-sign with Sea FM. I agreed to commit to another three years on the Central Coast with The Bree and Gawndy Show. I should have felt relieved to have finally made a decision, but as soon as my pen left the paper I regretted signing that bloody contract. A phone call later that night from Jase (you know, Jase from the Jase and PJ show) really threw me into a shitstorm of a problem. He told me I'd be crazy not to grab the ZM opportunity.

He said, 'Mate, you're making a big mistake if you don't take this chance.' Jase told me that Australian radio execs never take a chance on young broadcasters and that I risked being stuck in the provincial radio market forever. 'You could be there for the next ten years and never end up doing anything bigger. I'm telling you, New Zealand is a good place for you to grow as an announcer.'

It was a big moment for me, being given career advice from a guy I'd looked up to for such a long time. I trusted Jase's opinion — he was an Aussie like me and *he'd* made the leap across the ditch for a career opportunity so he knew exactly what he was talking about. I knew now what I needed to do. Staying in Australia was the safe option, but if I didn't grab the ZM opportunity I would always wonder what could have been. Even if it turned out to be a massive fucking disaster, I knew I'd regret it more if I didn't have the guts to give it a shot.

Even Mum, who if she had her way would have all her adult children living under her roof till she's 100, agreed it was

A LEAP OF FAITH

something I had to try.

All this was good and well, but stupid idiot indecisive Bree had re-signed the contract with Sea FM, hadn't she? I didn't know how I was going to get out of that. 'Just be brave, Brianna, and talk to them. I'm sure they'll be understanding,' said Mum, when I was freaking out to her down the phone.

Mumma Di was not correct on this occasion. When I told my boss I had decided to take a job in New Zealand, there was no sign of 'understanding'. He was absolutely livid that I'd changed my mind after signing the contract. He flipped his lid, telling me I was burning my bridges with Australian radio and I was unlikely to get work there ever again. It was a horrible way to finish what had been a really happy two years. To his credit, I bumped into him a few years later at a concert in Auckland and he apologised for having been a dick. He also told me I'd made the right decision for me and he was proud of how well I was doing.

***

A few months later there I was, getting off a plane in Auckland to begin my new life, a life where I knew no one and no one knew me. It should be noted that I am not a natural adventurer. I prefer to feel safe and settled, so uprooting my life like that was an enormous leap out of my comfort zone. And it turned out I underestimated what was involved in setting up in an entirely new country. I had to find somewhere to live, buy furniture, set up bank accounts, electricity, internet, a phone, buy a car, get a driver's licence . . . My to-do list was completely overwhelming and I didn't have anyone to ask for help. My girlfriend at the time, Ash, joined me in Auckland after a while, but our relationship was rocky to say the least and her presence only added to my stress.

At the start, work wasn't great either. Clint Roberts, a brilliant radio host from The Edge, had been confirmed as my co-host but the terms of his old contract meant he couldn't start the new show for six months. He was on gardening leave when I arrived in New Zealand — great for him, because who wouldn't want to get paid to not work? But it was bat-shit boring for me because I was left twiddling my thumbs. I went into the ZM offices each day to help out here and there, but there really wasn't much to do. For someone who feels awkward at the best of times, being the new girl at a workplace with pretty much zero purpose made it a hundred times worse. I was a spare prick at a wedding. The days moved at a snail's pace and I felt like I was stuck in limbo. Auckland was okay, I was slowly getting used to my new city, and the people at ZM were lovely, but I missed being on-air.

It was a tough time, but there was one shining light and that light's name was Cam Mansel, host of ZM's night show, who would become one of the best friends I'd ever had. We met for the first time in the lobby of the Rydges Hotel in Rotorua, where we were staying for a ZM music festival. The first thing I noticed about Cam was his giant Hollywood smile. If you were to google

TOP ME, DAD AND AMBER. MUM LOVED TEASING OUR HAIR TO WITHIN AN INCH OF ITS LIFE.

BOTTOM LEFT LITTLE ATHLETICS HIGH-JUMP CHAMPION. HARD TO BELIEVE GRAVITY WAS MY FRIEND BACK THEN.

BOTTOM RIGHT YEAR 9 SCHOOL PHOTOS — BEST IN SHOW. MY MUM SHOULD HAVE A CRIMINAL RECORD FOR LETTING ME LEAVE THE HOUSE IN THIS STATE.

TOP LEFT AGE 1 — LOVED A MATCHING SET, IT'S GIVING VOGUE!

TOP RIGHT FIRST DAY OF SCHOOL — AMBER, ADEN AND ME. LOVE THAT I CHOSE AN APPROPRIATE WICKER SANDAL FOR THE OCCASION.

BOTTOM GO BEAVERS! ONE OF THE MANY SOCCER TEAMS WHERE I WAS THE TALLEST AND ONE OF THE ONLY GIRLS.

TOP NONNO AND NONNA — RUMOUR HAS IT TAYLOR SWIFT WROTE HER SONG 'LOVE STORY' ABOUT THESE TWO.

BOTTOM LEFT BURLEIGH HEADS WITH NAN AND PA. THEY ALWAYS TOOK US ON THE BEST ADVENTURES AND DRESSED US IN RIDICULOUS MATCHING OUTFITS.

BOTTOM RIGHT AT AGE 8 I WAS OBSESSED WITH SHANIA TWAIN. NAN, WHO WAS QUITE THE SEAMSTRESS, MADE THIS 'THAT DON'T IMPRESS ME MUCH' OUTFIT COMPLETELY FROM SCRATCH!

TOP LEFT MUM AND ME — THE ORIGINAL MCLEOD'S DAUGHTERS.

TOP RIGHT AGE 15 — OFF TO A NEON-THEMED SCHOOL DANCE TO AWKWARDLY STAND IN THE CORNER AND WATCH MY FRIENDS GET PASH RASH.

BOTTOM MY BROTHER ADEN'S WEDDING DAY — AUNTY JULIE, SISTER AMBER, DAD, AUNTY SHIRL, ADEN, SISTER-IN-LAW KIM, ME AND MUM.

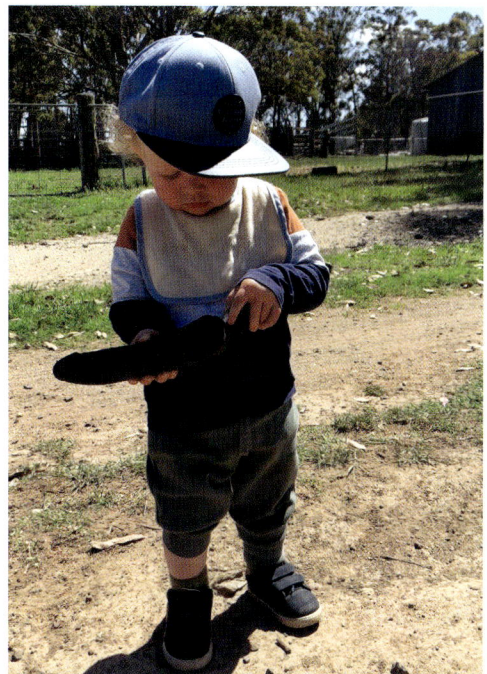

TOP LEFT FRIENDS AND A WINERY TOUR — ONLY THE ESSENTIALS. SOPHIA, DAN, MUM, KIM, ALLAN.

TOP RIGHT MY NEPHEW JONTI AND THE BIG BLACK DILLY HE FOUND IN THE PADDOCK.

BOTTOM THE BREE AND CLINT SHOW CHASED CHANNING TATUM IN LA. SPOILER — WE NEVER FOUND HIM . . . BUT PROBABLY SHOULD HAVE HAD A RESTRAINING ORDER TAKEN OUT AGAINST US. BEN, ME, CLINT, ELLIE.

TOP MATT CHISHOLM AND I ON SET FOR CELEBRITY TREASURE ISLAND — I WAS BATTLING SEVERE HUMIDI-TITTY

BOTTOM LEFT MUMMA DI, BIG STEVE AND BIG STEVE'S MOUSTACHE.

BOTTOM RIGHT AMBER'S WEDDING — THE COWBOY BOOTS GAVE ME BLISTERS.

TOP LEFT FRIENDS AND FESTIVALS — SOPHIA, CAM, JORDAN, GILLIAN, MEGAN.

TOP RIGHT BATHTUB FULL OF FROOT LOOPS. LOCKDOWN MADE SOME PEOPLE DRINK; I WAS DOING THIS.

BOTTOM ME AND SOPHIA. TALK ABOUT PUNCHING ABOVE MY WEIGHT!

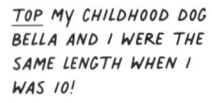

TOP MY CHILDHOOD DOG BELLA AND I WERE THE SAME LENGTH WHEN I WAS 10!

BOTTOM LEFT ME, SOPHIA AND THE GIRLS MERYL AND WHITNEY AT HOT WATER BEACH. WE ALL PEE'D IN THE SEA.

BOTTOM RIGHT WHITNEY HOUSTON AND MERYL STREEP.

'perfect smile', it's Cam's that would pop up. But it wasn't only his perfect teeth — there was something about this ridiculously good-looking human that almost stopped me in my tracks. Mum was with me (she'd come to stay because she knew I was struggling), and she felt the same — we both loved Cam straight away. He had this contagious energy that you don't come across every day, almost like a Jack Russell puppy. We gravitated to each other immediately and became instant friends.

Cam is a classic example of the 'chosen family' concept. He and I both being gay, we share an understanding and a deep connection. And over the years we have become each other's biggest support, riding the highs and lows of life together. We talk every day, see each other most weekends, and he's someone I can confidently say will be in my life forever. I have never had a friendship like it.

While Cam didn't seem to mind my Aussie-ness, it was dawning on me that a lot of Kiwis really didn't like Australians. Of course I was aware of the classic Aussie–Kiwi rivalry, but I'd always thought it was just a bit of fun, and we were like brothers and sisters who loved each other deep down. But no, I kept coming across Kiwis who genuinely hated Australia and Australians. When one of the Aussie-haters heard my accent or I told them where I was from, a look passed over their faces like they'd stood in dog shit and the conversation ended abruptly. As the start date for our first show was approaching, I couldn't help but worry about how me being Australian was going to go down with listeners. My job was to make people like me enough to choose to listen to me. I couldn't turn off my thick country Queensland accent or pretend I was from somewhere else; I just had to hope they could look past it. This Aussie bogan had her work cut out for her, I knew that.

I also knew that for the first time in my professional life, I was not going to hide my sexuality. I'd spent too long concealing that part of me, so when I took the ZM job, I promised myself I would be honest and authentic about who I am. But now this was freaking me out, too — was New Zealand ready for a queer Australian in their earholes? I imagined being chased back to Queensland by an angry mob of pitchfork-wielding Kiwi homophobes.

I know it might seem confusing that I was prepared to be open about my sexuality on radio while still keeping it a secret from Dad. But when I deep-dive on that now, I realise there were two parts to my thinking. The first was the knowledge that Dad was unlikely to ever hear it. While Mum listened to ZM religiously (streaming it at home each afternoon), I knew Dad didn't. He was so busy on the farm, it was unlikely he'd bother listening after he got home from work each day. But the second part was that if for some reason he *did* happen to hear me being open, then fuck it — I was fine with that. Part of me was desperate for Dad to have to face up to who I was, so maybe subconsciously I hoped that would happen.

On the home front, things weren't good with Ash, who wasn't enjoying Auckland. I felt under pressure to make her happy when all I really wanted to be doing was focusing on my work. Clint and

A LEAP OF FAITH

I were determined to start with a bang and were working hard on putting together content in time for our first show. Ash and I broke up the night before I was due to fly to Taiwan to interview Paul Rudd and Evangeline Lilly, who were promoting their film *Ant-Man* 2. Landing this junket was a big deal because we were planning to use it in our first show. I knew I needed to do a good job, but I was an emotional wreck of a human after the break-up, which hadn't been what you'd call amicable.

I boarded the plane, sat down in my seat, and cried the entire way. I felt so lost. I was living in a different country, far away from my family, and I hadn't been doing the thing I loved most in the world, which was being on-air. Now my relationship had ended and I felt like crap. I turned up to the interviews looking like dog shit. I'd been crying for 24 hours straight and hadn't slept a wink. I can't even remember how the interviews went, but afterwards I knew what needed to be done. Dinner was planned with a big group of PR people from Disney, who'd organised the junket. I sat down at the table, announced that I'd just broken up with my girlfriend, and we all agreed the only thing for it was to get shit-faced. We ripped into the booze in a big way.

I was feeling great until I remembered I had a plane to catch for my night flight home. I ran out of the restaurant, flagged down a taxi and made it to the airport just in time. I was as drunk as sin when I got there, but I wasn't too drunk to realise that the flight I was booked on transited through Brisbane. Without thinking, I marched up to the check-in desk and told the attendant I would be getting off in Brisbane. I told the lady I would arrange my own way back to Auckland at a later date.

I needed to see my family; that's all there was to it. The airline people weren't happy, though. I'd already checked in, so my bag had been put on the plane and was tagged through to Auckland. They tried to charge me $600 to change. I refused to pay, and I don't know how I got them to agree — maybe they could see I was unhinged — but somehow I managed to convince them to get my bag off in Brisbane and go through Customs.

Mum was waiting for me at Brisbane Airport. I'd never been happier to see anyone. I looked a right mess and smelt even worse, but I ran to her, collapsed into her arms in the biggest hug, and cried. 'Oh, Brianna,' Mum said. 'You'll be okay. We'll look after you.'

I stayed at home for a week. While a big part of me didn't want to go back to my new life in Auckland, I knew I had to. When I did get back to my flat, Ash had moved out and gone back to Australia. There was not one trace of her. It was like she'd vaporised.

* * *

Finally, Clint's restraint of trade was up and we could actually begin the show. I'd had six months to prepare, but taking over a show as popular as Jase and PJ's was a terrifying prospect. Clint and I knew they were big shoes for us to fill. But we worked well together, me and Clint. We had a

A LEAP OF FAITH

natural chemistry and from day one, it didn't feel hard. In fact, it felt good. It was fun! I was back doing what I loved.

Don't get me wrong — I was shitting myself every day for the first three months. And I tried my best to avoid looking at the text machine too much. In Australia we didn't have a text machine — listeners had to phone in if they wanted to talk to us. But here, the text machine (a computer where messages from listeners popped up) meant that listeners who didn't want to speak on-air could still communicate with us. Most of the time the messages are lovely and funny and kind. But the text machine can also be a dark place. Can you imagine having rolling feedback about how you're doing your job flashing up in front of your eyes while you're actually doing your job in real time? Luckily, though, that angry mob never turned up and the listeners seemed to quite like what we were doing. The routine was good for me, and I was also making friends and beginning to feel like maybe this New Zealand lark might work out.

Six years on, Clint and I are a well-oiled machine. And even though we've been doing this for so long, there is still an element of a challenge, which is what keeps it fresh and exciting. The big challenge is to find new and engaging things to talk about each day and to ensure we're being creative and different and unique. People have so much available when it comes to choosing their entertainment. We literally all have little screens in our pockets that we can reach for the moment boredom threatens. So it's up to me and Clint to make sure our radio show is better than what's on those phones.

In telly, there are teams of people behind the content. In radio, it's up to us — the hosts — to come up with the content. It's up to us to get to know our listeners and figure out what they enjoy. I really believe that content selection is an art. We need to make sure we're delivering the right balance of topics that will appeal to our audience. We need to engage them and entertain them. The good thing is, we know pretty fast if something has worked or not by the number of people who call or text in. Sometimes we hit that sweet spot and have hundreds or even thousands of people keen to engage and share their stories. And that's where the buzz lies for me — I know we're not doing anything truly important, like saving lives or making history — but radio gives us an amazing platform to really connect with people. And every single day, when I put my headphones on and sit down in front of that microphone, I am acutely aware I am talking to real-life humans. Humans like you and me, who might be going through tough times, shit times, happy times — whatever. It feels to me like an incredible privilege to be with them for that little window of time. And if I can bring a little bit of joy or laughter into that window of time, then that's a win.

I'll admit, though, that when you've been doing radio for a long time, some days can be a grind. You can have creative burn-out where it feels almost impossible to drum up ideas. At times you can feel like you're lacking motivation. But I've always thought that the people who last the longest in this industry are the ones with true passion for the job. The ones who still wake up excited for what they might bring to air that day or for the connection they might make with even one listener. It's these connections that drive me and I love it when people spot me on the street and want to chat. I never begrudge giving them my time because, at the heart of it, I'm just so grateful that they're listening and enjoying what I do.

People always think it's the hosts who choose the music that's played on radio, but we have nothing to do with it. Song selection is someone else's whole job and it's a highly scientific, considered task. Songs are put into categories based on their popularity, with some being played once a week and others once an hour. For the listener, that's great because it means you have a good chance of hearing your favourite song when you turn on the radio. For the hosts, listening to the same fucking song over and over can be a punishment. It's like being water-boarded, with pop songs being the water penetrating every corner of your brain. And when radio announcers get together, we often talk about the music that's been absolutely ruined for us.

'Happy' by Pharrell Williams does not make me happy. In fact, I'd be happy if I never heard that song again. 'Blurred Lines' by that creep Robin Thicke . . . oh my god, I can't deal. If I hear *that* again I'll scream. 'Uptown Funk' is a shocker. 'Shake It Off' by Taylor Swift. Holy shit, what a punish — I've heard that approximately one million times too many. Then there are the songs we call wounders, the slow, sad songs that get played a lot. Benson Boone is responsible for a lot of wounders, but Lewis Capaldi is the official Wounder King. These miserable songs have the ability to bring the whole mood of the studio crashing down.

Clint and I might be talking about something really funny, then one of us will go 'here's Lewis Capaldi' and it's like a dark cloud descends.

Most days at work, though, I think, 'Fuck, this is cool.' If Clint and I get a good little segment going or a really great caller rings through and the text machine lights up, it feels great. I am constantly reminded about how amazing my job is and how fortunate I am to have a job I love.

Things happen in my life, and I think 'thank goodness I work on radio' because I have a platform to share them. Some stories are just too good not to share with the nation. Like when my two-year-old nephew Jonty found a big black dildo in the paddock at home. I mean, that's a story that shouldn't be kept to ourselves. I'd originally purchased this XL dildo for my sister's hens' party, because every good hens' party needs a big black dildo, right? I'd organised an R18 pass-the-parcel, with every layer containing something naughty. You should have seen Mum and her sisters cackling away as they opened the layers to find cock rings, whips, handcuffs and nipple tassels. The main prize, the *pièce de résistance* if you will, was this giant black dildo which my 70-year-old Aunty Shirley was lucky enough to win. She could hardly breathe for laughing when she laid eyes on that thing.

The dildo travelled everywhere with us during the party. It joined us for drinks at a bar and went on a riverboat cruise helmed by male strippers. Forget the bride-to-be — that dildo was the star of the show.

A LEAP OF FAITH

Fast-forward a few weeks, and on the night of my sister's wedding this giant black dildo rose again like Jesus. The wedding was held in a marquee on my parents' farm. I'd been very well behaved and appropriate performing my bridesmaid and speech-making duties. But when I popped back to the house for a wee, I noticed out of the corner of my eye that large rubber cock sitting on the bookshelf. I couldn't help myself; I knew that dildo needed another outing. Before long I was back in the marquee, interviewing guests with my big black dildo-microphone. My cousin Shane then got hold of it and started throwing it around the dance floor like a grenade. Not all brides would be keen to have a dildo make an appearance on their special day, but luckily Amber has a great sense of humour and happily joined in the dildo fun.

At some point in the night, the dildo must have been discarded because it wasn't seen again. Until one lovely, wholesome afternoon four years later when Mumma Di took her adorable grandson to feed the sheep in the paddock outside their house. 'Look, Nin-Nin — I found something!' Thank goodness she had the presence of mind to snap a photo of that angelic wee boy holding this giant rubber dick. Mumma Di knew she had to capture this moment of pure hilarity.

Do you like maths?

After my horrible break-up with Ash, I swore off dating for a while. I felt like I'd been through the wringer emotionally and I certainly wasn't in the right frame of mind to go out looking for a new relationship. And I knew I needed to focus on the new job and settling into this New Zealand life.

But it didn't take long till I was bored at home on my own after work each night, so I minced my way back on to the dating apps. I had no intention of going on any actual dates. I just wasted time scrolling through profiles, occasionally matching with someone, chatting for a bit and moving on to the next one. One of the women I matched with on Bumble was called Sophia. She was a nurse from Auckland and I thought she looked cute. She had dark hair and a lovely smile so I thought, 'Fuck it, I'll message her.'

DO YOU LIKE MATHS?

The normal course of action here would be to say something along the lines of, 'Hi, how are you?' Not me, though. For some inexplicable reason, I typed these words:

'Do you like maths?'

Five years later, Sophia still hasn't let me live this down. And yes, it was the worst opening line in the history of dating apps. I didn't even say 'hi' or 'hello' at the start! I don't know *what* I was thinking. I guess I was so uninterested in meeting someone that I didn't give a shit if I sounded like a dick. And in my defence, I do think a person's interest in maths says a lot about their personality. If you love maths, you're probably very smart, very organised, very well paid, and possibly a bit . . . boring?

Sophia wrote back: 'Um, maths is okay I guess.'

I knew she was judging me. She was thinking, 'Who is this weirdo?' I am amazed she didn't just block me. We chatted for a while, added each other on Instagram, but after a week or so the conversation fizzled out and that was that. I didn't really think about her again until seven months later when I took myself to the Philippines for an *Eat Pray Love*-style journey of self-discovery. Kidding — I just needed a holiday. I met up with friends in El Nido, a beautiful beach town on Palawan Island. The trip revolved around lying on the beach, swimming in the incredible tropical ocean and drinking cheap cocktails. It was heaven, apart from a bad case of spitty-bum from the nasty tap water. Strangely, I decided to interrupt this mostly blissful regimen by choosing to climb Taraw Peak — a big, jagged mountain — in the middle of the night. With just a tiny torch for light and a random dude from the village as my guide, I set out at 4 a.m. to get to the top in time for sunrise. This was no casual bush trail. It was a terrifying climb up a cliff over jagged rocks in extreme humidity. It was the hardest thing my body has ever dealt with, and when I reached the top and the sun came up, I looked down and nearly passed out. I had climbed a sheer rock face in old trainers, with no safety equipment and no light. If I'd slipped, I would have been a goner. But I made it — so of course I took a selfie of me at the top with the amazing view below and shared it on the 'gram because, you know, have you even *had* a death-defying experience in a foreign country if it's not on your grid?

A few hours later, a message from Sophia appeared in my DMs. She'd seen my photo and told me she'd done the same trip a year earlier. She shared some recommendations of places to see and things to do in El Nido for the rest of my time there. And from that moment, we just started chatting again. When I arrived back in New Zealand a week later, we continued chatting. We chatted some more till, finally, maybe a month or two later, we went on our first date at a bar on K-Road called Lovebucket.

As soon as we sat down together, the conversation was easy. I wouldn't say it was love at first sight, because what sort of idiot believes in that shit? But there was an ease between us. We both felt comfortable with each other, and while we both knew we liked each other, neither of us wanted to rush into anything — which is quite unusual for a pair of lesbians.

Question: What does a lesbian bring on a second date? Answer: A U-Haul.

DO YOU LIKE MATHS?

The stereotype of U-Haul lesbians refers to gay women's tendencies to get serious fast. As the joke goes, we fall in love at breakneck speed and move in with each other after a couple of dates. I have definitely been guilty of this. There were times where I was so completely infatuated with a woman that it led to some not-very-well-thought-out decisions.

There was no denying that I liked Sophia, though. I *really* liked her. She was different to anyone I'd ever met. And I was impressed by her. While I was telling fart jokes on the radio for a living, she was literally saving tiny little lives in the hospital as a nurse at the Neonatal Intensive Care Unit. How cool is that? She was funny — not as funny as me, but still funny — and she laughed at my jokes. We shared the same values. We loved our families, took our friendships seriously, and we'd both been through the ups and downs of coming out slowly and painfully during our twenties. But it wasn't until I was away filming my first season of *Celebrity Treasure Island* (more on this later) that our relationship jumped up a gear. I rang her every single day from on location in Fiji and she became a really important source of support and comfort to me. I could tell her exactly how I was feeling — about my sense of inadequacy, the crippling nerves, the exhaustion — and also all the fun stuff, too. She was an absolute rock.

When I got back, I went straight from the airport to her place. After that, we were inseparable. And for the first time in years, I felt completely settled and happy. There was no game-playing, no mystery, no second-guessing about where we each stood. We liked each other and were there for each other and, most importantly, it felt like we were on the same level when it came to the things that were important — friendship, family and being good to other people.

* * *

Stories about a weird illness called coronavirus had been floating around for a while, but neither Sophia or I really thought it would impact little old New Zealand. We'd booked a trip to Bali and were excited to travel together for the first time. But in March 2020, a few weeks before we were due to fly out, New Zealand went into lockdown. Covid-19 was knocking on our door and Prime Minister Jacinda Ardern wasn't bloody having it! In that instant, the world changed and Sophia and I, who were living in separate flats, were faced with the prospect of not being able to see each other. This felt serious; we were imagining armoured vehicles patrolling the streets and soldiers inspecting our 'bubbles' for imposters. We had to make decisions fast about whether we tried to live together or could manage apart. Not knowing if it was the right thing to do, we decided to give living together a shot and Sophia moved into the flat I shared with my friends Allan and Annabelle. It was a huge turning point in our relationship. Not only were we watching history unfold as Covid-19 spread around the world, we were also realising the two of us had something really special.

DO YOU LIKE MATHS?

While most people couldn't leave their homes during lockdown, Sophia was still working at the hospital with the little babies every day and I was going off to do my radio show, because broadcasting was also on the list of essential services. When we got home we would return to normal lockdown activities, like excessive any-time-of-the-day-or-night drinking, board games, *Monopoly Deal* tournaments and Zoom quizzes. Another good thing about having Sophia with us was that she could skip the queues at the supermarket just by showing her nurse badge, so we made her do all the shopping. 'That's the only reason we're letting you stay,' we'd joke.

When lockdown was lifted seven weeks later, Sophia and I both knew we didn't want to go back to living apart, so we moved into her place permanently.

Dating in the lesbian world can be a bit messy sometimes. The pool of available women is smaller, so the risk of crossover is higher — it's not unusual to find one of your friends dating your ex, which can feel a bit weird. With Sophia, though, neither of us had any baggage like that and, for once, we didn't have anything hard to navigate. We trusted each other from the very start, which in my opinion is what every good relationship needs. Sophia gave me the security and love I had been searching for and longing for my whole life.

Don't get me wrong — we're not perfect and we have plenty of bust-ups. But they're never about anything major. We never disagree over the big stuff.

Here are the reasons why I love Sophia:

1. She is a deathly loyal human being. Once you have Sophia on your side, she's there for life and she will never, ever let you down.
2. She is a genuinely good person. Every single day I see her do lovely things for others. She's a great friend, a great sister and a great daughter, and she puts everyone before herself.
3. She laughs at all my jokes. Even when they're not very good ones.

Now, here are the three things I love her IN SPITE OF:

1. She hangs the toilet roll the wrong way. For years I thought we were engaged in a silent war over which way the paper should hang because I thought everyone knew it must hang down the front of the roll. It turned out that Sophia didn't even know it was a thing. That is some psychopathic shit. Now I think she hangs it the wrong way just to piss me off.
2. In the bathroom, we have one towel rail. Ever since we've lived together, my towel hangs on the top rail and hers is on the bottom. But every single day, Sophia washes her hands after using the toilet and then dries her hands ON MY TOWEL. Why would she do this? It drives me insane because it means my towel is always

damp and — worse — it means I'm drying my nice clean cooch fresh from the shower where her filthy wet hands have been.
3. And, Sophia never lets me take the toothpaste when I go away on a trip. This is not right. The person who is at home can easily go to a store and buy another tube, but it's harder for the person travelling. Am I right or am I right? Perhaps not, but this is how I see into it.

Other than these three areas for improvement, Sophia is the perfect partner and I thank my lucky stars every day that I have her. She is absolutely a better person than me. She mows the lawns, builds the flat-pack furniture, pays the bills, understands how mortgages work, is mentally stable and hasn't dumped me even when I'm an anxious mess, irrational and impossible in the grip of a mental breakdown. Sophia is the captain of our ship while I'm a pretty crappy first mate. I love her — she puts up with me, this absolutely messy troll of a human being.

Sophia just accepts me for me. Even this book is a good example. Sophia is a private person. I am sure she would prefer I had a job that didn't involve me revealing our secrets to hundreds of thousands of people each week. But she accepts who I am and even lets me write about her.

* * *

UNAPOLOGETICALLY ME

When we first got together, I had to explain to Sophia that while I was 'mostly' out, there was one teeny little issue: I still hadn't managed to talk to my dad about this giant fucking elephant in the room. Of course by then he must have known I was queer — I was in my thirties, for god's sake — but he hadn't raised it with me and I hadn't said anything either. It sounds crazy that this situation had continued for so long, but Sophia didn't judge me for any of it or pressure me to change it. She knew very well that coming out to your family isn't always a box of Roses.

It's now Christmas 2019. I'm 30 and been pretty much exclusively in relationships with women for over a decade, yet I'm still keeping it a secret from my dad. Fucked up, I know. I travel home from New Zealand for Christmas, and at New Year Sophia — my girlfriend, the woman I can see a future with — is coming to join us.

'Brianna's friend Sophia is coming to stay,' I hear Mum say to Dad. Friend. What a farce.

Sophia arrives, is warmly welcomed by everyone (including Dad), and she shares my room and my bed. There's no doubt in my mind that everyone in my family knows that Sophia is much more than just a friend to me, but we all play along with this silly 'let's pretend Brianna's straight' game. Everyone is lovely to Sophia. She fits in so easily and everyone loves her. She plays with my nephew, laughs with Mum and banters with Dad. We cook together, eat together, go on long walks on the farm. We are a couple. It is *so bloody obvious*.

DO YOU LIKE MATHS?

After a few days at the farm, Amber comes to me. 'I really like Sophia,' she says. 'You should invite her home more often.' This is a huge thing — I know now that my big sister, who I've always looked up to and wanted to make proud, is acknowledging and accepting me for who I am. It feels like one of the most special moments I'd ever had with my sister. We're not super-affectionate with each other, or people who talk about their feelings a lot together, but this moment means so much to me. It might seem small, but for me it is enormously significant.

Now it is just Dad who can't seem to face reality. And even then, I truly believe it might never happen.

But on the day we're due to leave, Sophia and I are in my bedroom packing up our bags and getting organised. Dad walks in, clears his throat, and says, 'It's been really nice having you girls to stay.' He looks emotional and I suddenly realise what's happening. Oh my god, he's going to fucking say something! I can't believe it.

'Can I talk to you for a moment, Brianna?' he asks, motioning for me to step out into the hallway with him. We step out of the room, and I can't help it but I'm bloody crying already.

'I'm very proud of you, Brianna. And I'm so happy that you found someone as lovely as Sophia.'

Dad hugs me, kisses me, and tells me again how proud he is of me. 'I think you're very brave for being able to be yourself,' he says. 'I think you're so brave for being who you are in your work and in your life. I know it's been hard for you but I love you, and being gay doesn't change any of that.'

There it was — the acknowledgement of what had been locked away for so long. The secret was out. It was a short conversation, but Dad said what he'd been unable to say for years: that he loved me no matter what, and that he supported me. I was crying my eyes out. I have never felt so emotional about anything in my life. And it was nice. It was nice that he finally talked to me and told me he loved me no matter what.

Mum later told me that she'd finally snapped that morning. She couldn't bear the fact Dad hadn't faced up to what had been so obvious for so long, and she couldn't understand how he couldn't comprehend *why* it was important to bring it out into the open. I think he'd hoped it could stay locked away in the too-hard box forever.

I was proud of Dad for finally telling me he loved me and it was okay. But niggling at the back of my mind were the questions: 'What took you so long? Where was this acceptance eight or ten years ago?' I've spent a lot of time thinking about this since, and I know now he didn't have a clue what his silence was doing to me. At the start, he couldn't accept that his daughter was gay. He had to work through all that religious and cultural brainwashing and learn to come to terms with who I was. At first he found it hard to accept, hard to know what to say to me — so for him, it was easier to say nothing. He didn't know that in my eyes, his silence translated as judgement. He didn't realise that pushing it to the too-hard pile had caused me real and lasting damage. He didn't know that I genuinely feared he would never love me if he found out who I really was.

I am very aware that I was a big part of the secret-keeping, because it was me who begged Mum never to tell him. But I was young when I made that decision. I was lost and I didn't know what I was doing. I didn't realise the seriousness of not being true to myself and the damage that would cause. And I truly didn't think it would go on for so long. I'm not angry at Mum, because she was being loyal, but I do wish she'd made the call that this was perhaps not the best approach. I learned the hard way that secrecy equals shame. And shame leads to all sorts of shit, like feeling like you don't belong, that there's something inherently wrong with you.

I should have bloody talked to him about it years ago.

Sophia is part of the family now. And our relationship is there for all to see. Mum, Dad, Amber and Aden love us both. And Dad sees we are no different to my sister and her husband, and my brother and his wife. Dad is our go-to for DIY advice and he flies over when we need help with the yard — sometimes everyone needs a bit of man-power in the house! At Aden's wedding, Dad sat alongside us in the pew, introducing Sophia as my partner to the conservative old biddies sitting behind us. And he kept his head held high as the smiles left their faces quicker than the speed of light. Those moments make me sad for Dad, but he's here for us and proud of us and I am so thankful we got there in the end.

Little Terramoto

Back when I was at school, all my reports went along the lines of 'Brianna is too easily distracted', 'Brianna needs to focus more', 'Brianna could achieve more if she put more effort in', 'Brianna needs to stop distracting others'. There were plenty of good comments, too, but the overriding theme was my lack of ability to concentrate and stay on task. I was the class clown. The one who made everyone laugh. That cheeky kid who would talk back to the teachers but get away with it because it was good-humoured, not mean.

I wanted to do well, and I wanted to listen and learn. But no matter how hard I tried, my mind would wander. I would look at the other kids, sitting there quietly following instructions and doing their work, and I'd think, 'How can they do that?' Sometimes it felt physically impossible for me to concentrate, like there were ten televisions turned on at once inside my brain and I had to figure out which one to focus on — as well as trying to follow along with the teacher. It was a hopeless task. Trying to single out the important thoughts and messages from all the ones that were flying around inside my head was exhausting and overwhelming.

At home it was all 'look at meeeeee!', and I needed constant action. Mum says I was entertaining, but I know the 'Little Terramoto' nickname meant a bit more than that. Sure I was funny and full of energy, but I was also irritating. I was forever being reminded to use my 'inside voice'. I had zero patience; I couldn't wait my turn for things. I didn't mean to be rude, but I found it really hard not to interrupt or push in. I had such a short fuse. Once I'd had my explosion I'd carry on as normal.

I did really well at primary school because it was tiny and I got the attention my chaotic brain needed. But at high school it was a different matter. My teachers at high school knew I couldn't concentrate, so they adapted things to suit me. When the class was reading *To Kill A Mockingbird*, I was put in another room to watch the movie instead. I still haven't ever managed to read a book from start to finish (apart from this one, of course). In the subjects I enjoyed, like PE, drama and English, I did well. It was the subjects like maths and science that I found soul-destroyingly boring; I simply could not listen or concentrate. So I never bothered even trying.

∗ ∗ ∗

'Have you ever thought about getting assessed for ADHD?' read the text message from my friend Ellie Harwood.

What? Me? ADHD? Isn't that what nine-year-old boys who can't sit still at school have? 'I don't have ADHD,' I thought. I put my phone down on my desk at ZM and went back to what I was doing, thinking 'I'll deal with that one later.' (I didn't yet know it, but that was a classic ADHD move right there — putting things off for as long as possible.)

Ellie was a colleague at ZM. She was one of the first people I really hit it off with when I moved to New Zealand, and her friendship was a lifeline when I was feeling awkward and out of place as the new girl. We shared the same weird sense of humour and we seemed to experience life in really similar ways. We always ended up laughing at some aspect of how shit we both were as humans. Ellie and I knew what it felt like to be awkward in social and work situations and we shared a sense of disbelief that we were managing to make it through each day as adults. Ellie was no stranger to anxiety, either, and we became each other's go-to person when we were struggling. We'd talk each other off whatever emotional cliff we were teetering on that day.

While everyone around us seemed to have their shit together, we were all over the bloody show. We seemed to struggle with normal adult things, like paying bills on time, sorting out taxes, even keeping our house or desk tidy. We were Queens of Procrastination and left our work till the last minute. I always joked about how I was only hanging on by the skin of my teeth and finally I'd met someone who was the same. It was so nice to find a friend who was dealing with the same stuff as me.

Ellie was also the only other person I knew who got as much joy out of fart jokes and toilet humour as I did. There are two types of people in this world: those who find farts funny, and those who lie and say they don't. Farts ARE funny. But there is an annoying double-standard where boys can fart and everyone laughs, but when girls do it, it's gross. I had been tackling that sexism head-on (arse-on?) ever since I was little, farting my way through primary school, high school, university and now the workplace. I loved nothing more than seeing people's reactions when I dropped a stink bomb in a majorly inappropriate setting.

The reactions were so good that I decided to start filming them. Before long, I had a splendid montage of fart footage. Loud ones, quiet ones, high-pitched ones, low-pitched ones, long ones, short ones . . . every fart you could imagine was featured. And every type of response was captured, too. I thought long and hard about posting it. Was it a step too far? Would my followers be repulsed and block me? Or would they find it as funny as I did? I went to Ellie for advice.

'What do you think? Is this too gross for the internet?'

Ellie was laughing so hard she could barely get her words out. 'The world needs to see this,' she said. I didn't require any more encouragement and popped it up on Facebook and Instagram. Ellie was right: people bloody loved it and the fart video went crazy viral. People sometimes ask me if I get embarrassed. Not really. If it's funny, that's good enough for me.

At first Ellie was working in the online team, but she was super-talented and I was always telling her she should be doing more. After a while, she started popping into the studio and did bits and pieces with me and Clint, and then she became our social-media producer and then our full-time producer, which meant we were spending even more time together than before. But in the three years we worked together, the idea that one of us might have ADHD never came up.

'I've just been diagnosed, and I think you should look into it, too,' Ellie messaged.

I tried to put that text out of my mind, but it wasn't easy. If Ellie had gone to get help, did that mean I should too? I had always felt there was something different with me. Could this be it? I called Ellie, and she told me all about her ADHD journey. She said she'd started taking meds and they'd made her feel much better. 'Life feels easier,' she said. 'There's less chaos.'

I hit up Dr Google. I don't know how I'd missed it, but information about ADHD (attention deficit hyperactivity disorder) was everywhere, and it became pretty clear that this neurological condition was not uncommon. I read that the ADHD brain develops at a slower rate to typical people's brains and that the frontal lobe is differently wired. This is important because that's the part that's in charge of attention, behaviour, emotion, energy or motor control, judgement and executive function. Executive function means the skills you need to have your shit together. You know, the ability to organise yourself and your stuff and your time.

I scanned lists of ADHD traits and symptoms, and for the first time in my life I felt like I might have finally cracked the mystery of what was different about me.

'Acts as though driven by a motor.' *Tick.*

'Struggles with focus and concentration.' *Tick.*

'Difficulty with time management.' *Tick.*

'Disorganisation.' *Tick.*

'Procrastination.' *Tick.*

'Feeling overwhelmed.' *Tick.*

'Anxiety.' *Tick.*

'Restlessness.' *Tick.*

Trawling the internet like a maniac, I stayed up all night reading stories about women who'd been diagnosed as adults. Girls with ADHD often go undiagnosed until adulthood, while boys are more likely to get help earlier. Until recently, girls and women with ADHD have been woefully neglected, and let down by the lack of research and interest in how ADHD presents in females. I learned that girls with ADHD often do something called 'masking', where they learn to cover up their ADHD symptoms in order to fit in. That felt familiar. I'd spent most of my teenage years trying to be 'normal', whatever *that* was. All I wanted was to be like everyone else, but so often I was stuck with this sense that I just wasn't the same. That there was something about me that made me weird, awkward and annoying. My brain had always felt crazily busy. I'd always struggled to focus on just one thing, with thoughts running a mile a minute through my head every single minute of the day. I read page after page of other people's ADHD experiences, becoming more and more convinced that I too had ADHD. Maybe the parts of life I found hard weren't my fault? Maybe I wasn't just weird and useless? It felt like a revelation.

But because of who I am as a human, it took me a full year to go any further than simply reading about ADHD on the internet. Did I mention that procrastination is a classic ADHD trait? Putting things off was something I'd been doing my whole life. If ever there's something that feels hard to tackle, I can put that shit off for as long as possible. It might be the smallest thing, like registering my dog on the internet, yet it feels like an impossible task. And the longer I put it off, the bigger it feels.

Twelve months on, I finally made an appointment with the GP. I talked to her, and she agreed that ADHD was worth looking into. She referred me to a psychologist named Chris. I am always wary of new doctors or medical people, so I was a bag of nerves when I logged in for my appointment, which thanks to another fucking Covid lockdown was over Zoom. I had already filled out long questionnaires, Mum had done one too, and I'd sent off old school reports. I needn't have worried; Chris was lovely. We talked for almost an hour. Chris asked me about my childhood, my emotions, relationships, ability to cope at work, my ability to concentrate, family and everything else in between. One of the first things she said was, 'You've done so well despite everything you've had going on.' I felt like crying. It was like she was proud of me. And I could see that she understood what I meant by the chaos inside my head.

Finally, Chris told me she was sure I had ADHD. There are three types of ADHD, she explained: impulsive/hyperactive, inattentive, and combined. 'You meet the criteria for combined type ADHD.' This, she explained, meant I showed both inattention symptoms — which would explain why I found it so bloody hard to focus at school and university — and impulsive/hyperactive symptoms, which would account for my hectic brain. She also explained that there was a link between ADHD and anxiety and depression. She told me some people with ADHD show amazing intuition, meaning they see and feel everything — yet this can create a hyper-awareness that can make them feel anxious. ADHD people are often 'interest-driven', which basically means we can't do anything we find boring, but give us something we're interested in and we'll fucking *nail* it. The official term for this is hyper-focus.

This was the first time in my life I'd felt really understood. All the things I thought were different or negative about me might actually be linked to ADHD. It was quite a revelation.

Chris then talked to me about dopamine. 'Dopa-what?' I asked. Dopamine, she explained, is a neurotransmitter, a chemical messenger in the brain that is vital to our ability to function. Essentially, dopamine is what makes us feel good. But people with ADHD have lower levels of the stuff, which means we can struggle with motivation, focus and energy. It also means us ADHDers have to seek dopamine out. Some people turn to risky stuff like drugs or alcohol. I knew exactly what gave me my dopamine — playing sport, making people laugh, and doing my job. There's no bigger hit of dopamine than the one you get from the rush of being live on-air. Oh — and internet shopping. If I'm ever a bit low, I'll make a totally impulsive do-not-need-this purchase online and feel instantly better. I once bought a slushie machine off one of those irresistible Instagram sellers. 'Ooh, I could put alcohol in this and it'll be great for parties,' I told myself as I confirmed the purchase. Important note: I hardly ever throw parties.

Now that I had an ADHD diagnosis, I had to work out if I wanted to treat it. I could consider finding an ADHD coach to help me navigate the trickier parts of life, or I could try medication. Chris referred me to a psychiatrist, because only they can prescribe the drugs. It would be a three-month wait for an appointment.

Getting an ADHD diagnosis turned out to be a real mind-fuck and an emotional journey that I wasn't prepared for. I went into what I can only describe as a grieving process for who I thought I was. Neurotypical Bree was replaced by a neurodivergent version of myself and that was hard to get my head around. I felt angry because my whole life I'd been told that I was too much, not enough, this, that and the other, only to discover a lot of it was all out my control anyway. Interestingly, the diagnosis made me consider my entire life through a different lens. I started to go through memories with a new perspective. It sounds weird, but it was like rewatching a movie I'd seen a million times but with a much deeper understanding of the plot.

LITTLE TERRAMOTO

* * *

In the meantime, I had to tell Mum and Dad.

'I've got ADHD,' I said down the phone.

They hit the roof. 'Don't be ridiculous, there's nothing wrong with you!' said Mum. 'I don't believe it,' said Dad.

I get it — they didn't want to acknowledge that their daughter was anything less than perfect. But it was annoying, because it meant it was now up to me to convince them. Luckily that didn't take long; all I had to do was run them through the symptoms and they could see that the diagnosis made sense. Mum was realising that the things about me she'd always thought were just Brianna-isms were actually a bit more complicated. My legendary tantrums, which could be sparked by something so small, were likely related to the emotional dysregulation that most people with ADHD experience. Mum remembered me having major meltdowns over tiny things, and huge sensitivity. If I didn't think my homework was good enough, I'd cry and scream and refuse to go to school. And I needed to know exactly what the day's plan was, otherwise I'd refuse to take part. I could flip my lid, say nasty things, and five minutes later it was like it never happened. What Mum was describing was a very typical picture of a child with ADHD.

Embarrassingly, my hot temper has not gone away with adulthood and I am ashamed to admit to still having the occasional adult tantrum. The last shocker was when I was travelling in Italy with my parents. We were at the Colosseum, for god's sake — a bucket-list historical site — yet I had to ruin it with a hissy fit. At age 33. The tour, which was meant to last two-and-a-half hours, went on for *four* and it felt like the guide was never, ever going to stop talking. I got frustrated. It was a hot day, hot as Satan's arsehole, the kind of hot where you get chafing between your thighs. I got frustrated. I was raging internally. I couldn't handle my irritation, and eventually erupted, hissed at my parents 'this is bullshit' and stormed off.

An hour later, after a sit-down and a cold beer, I apologised to my parents. I felt so embarrassed. There is nothing cool about losing your shit at your parents at that age, but at least now I was beginning to understand that these sorts of flip-outs (or my emotional dysregulation, as Chris the psychologist called it) could be an ADHD thing, too.

Mum went away and did lots of her own reading, and the first thing that happened was she was hit with a shit-ton of mum guilt. She felt terrible for not recognising I had something like this going on and wished she'd known about ADHD when I was a child and a teenager so she could have got me some help. She knows my school life could have been a lot easier if they'd known what was going on. I don't blame her, though. No one had a clue what ADHD was back then and barely any girls were getting diagnosed in the '90s.

✱ ✱ ✱

I was excited to try ADHD meds because I thought it might be a magic bullet that would instantly transform me. I would take this little pill and be a whole new person. But my appointment with the psychiatrist didn't go well. I sat down opposite her, feeling nervous but hopeful. Her first line of questioning threw me: 'Have you ever thought about harming yourself?' 'Have you had suicidal thoughts?'

I wasn't prepared for this — I was not suicidal and I was not depressed. I was here to discuss my ADHD diagnosis and treatment plan. Instead, I felt like I was back in Stanthorpe after the home invasion being forced to talk about scary topics that didn't relate to me at all. I felt trapped in that office, panic rising through my body and a desperate urge to make a run for the door.

As the doctor continued speaking, I became convinced she thought I was making this up, that I was just another person jumping on the ADHD bandwagon. I got the feeling she thought I was attention-seeking. It was a terrible feeling — and in that moment, sitting on that squishy chair with its wooden arms across from the psychiatrist in her beige-coloured little room, I began to doubt myself. Maybe I had made all this up. Did I really deserve help for this?

I sat through the rest of the consult, squeaking out one-word answers to her questions. Finally, we got to the reason why I'd gone to her. 'Would you like to try medication?'

'I'd like to try the meds if you think it could help,' I said, desperate to get out of there. She prescribed me a stimulant drug commonly used for ADHD. 'Try this and see how you go,' she said, handing over the piece of paper and ushering me out the door. There was no follow-up appointment or advice about side effects.

I left feeling confused and deflated. I walked into a bakery, bought myself an almond croissant and sat in my car, stuffing my face and crying, feeling like a proper loser. I marinated in my sadness for ten minutes before dusting off the croissant crumbs and heading into work. At lunchtime I went to a pharmacy and handed my prescription over. I felt exposed and embarrassed. Were they laughing at me? Was I being judged? I shoved the pack of pills in my bag, where they stayed for several weeks.

'When are you going to try them?' asked Sophia.

Good question. I was scared. I talked to my friend Jazz Thornton, who also happens to be an incredible mental-health advocate — plus she has ADHD. If anyone knows what they're on about with this stuff, it's her. Jazz suggested trying the meds for the first time during a weekend when I didn't have much on. Then I would have the time and space to really let myself notice their effects. So, one Sunday morning I decided it was time. I gulped the little white pill down with a glass of water and sat quietly waiting to be transformed into a whole new person. I didn't feel anything much, but for some mysterious reason I was overcome with the urge to clean out my bathroom vanity. I marched into the bathroom, got down on my knees and pulled everything out. Normally I would've given up then, left piles of crap all over the floor and walked away with plans to do it later. A later that would never come.

This time, though, I sorted through all the tubes and bottles I'd pulled out, throwing away all the half-used cosmetics I'd bought on dopamine-inducing internet-shopping sprees. I chucked the empty toothpaste tubes and dried-out lipsticks. I wiped down the filthy shelves stained with fake tan and foundation, and carefully put things back in. I was being neat and my vanity had never looked as good as it did that day.

Sophia stood at the door watching me. She was dumbfounded; she had never seen me start a domestic task with such vigour. And she had most definitely never seen me complete a domestic task so efficiently. Hooray! The drugs were working! I was a new person!

But the thing is, I wasn't a new person. It was a fluke. The next day, I took my little pill and went to work. I arrived at my desk, fired up my computer, and waited, listening intently to my brain and my body. I couldn't wait to feel that clarity and focus that had evaded me for so long, and I couldn't wait to see how it would affect me at work. But nothing happened. I felt no different. I was the same me. And when I went on-air, I was just the same as usual, too. Hmm, maybe the bathroom vanity was an anomaly. I tried again a few days later. Same again. No great focus or better concentration, and I was still ignoring texts and emails like always. I started to feel really disheartened. I thought these drugs were meant to help? I had really hoped the pills would be the instant fix I'd longed for. I tried again the next day, and the day after. Nothing. No change. After that, I didn't take the pills again.

Lots of people have told me since that perhaps I should try another type of ADHD drug, or a different dose of the one I was prescribed — and I guess they're right, I should give it another crack. I need to go back and talk to another doctor, and maybe I will. Oh, there's that ADHD again: putting things off.

I have a lot of shame about some of my ADHD traits. I'm trying to be kind to myself, but there are things I do and have done that make me feel bad for the people in my life. One of the worst is my inability to respond to messages in a timely fashion. If it's work-related, especially if there's pressure attached or decisions that need to be made, I will avoid dealing with it for as long as humanly possible. The email will arrive in my inbox, but the idea of writing back is overwhelming. Sometimes I won't even open an email or message because I've already started feeling stressed about having to respond. It doesn't make sense, because it's not like I find the actual writing of words hard, or the mechanics of my job difficult. But every message or email that lands in my inbox gives me a creeping sense of panic and guilt. If I don't attend to it right at that moment, then it's likely to sit there for days or weeks.

People who know me well have come to learn that they need to message me two, three or four times before they get a response. Right now, I have 476 unread texts sitting on my phone and 2160 unread emails. And as the messages pile up, the overwhelm increases and I become completely stuck. I can't do anything about it.

While I adore my friends, plenty of old friendships have

fizzled out because I can't seem to maintain the contact needed to sustain them, particularly if I live in a different city or country. I look at old school or uni friends who all still hang out and keep in touch, and wonder, 'How have you managed to do that?' It makes me feel a bit inadequate — am I not worth staying in touch with? But really I know it's a two-way thing; I haven't put the effort in either. And it's not because I don't want to or I don't value these people, it's just that I have limited energy to share with others. Over time, I have learned that I don't have enough room in my chaotic brain for what it takes to maintain a huge group of friends. And I'm okay with that. I'd rather be a good friend to a small circle than a shit friend to many.

This inability to get things done applies to my mental to-do list as well. I will put off a task for so long that my anxiety about it gets bigger and bigger and then my brain shuts down and I can't do anything about it. It's a horrible cycle, and often it relates to a very small task like filling in a form or putting away the washing after I've folded it.

The best way to describe what having ADHD is like is that my brain mirrors my laptop, with its 436 open tabs. It's as though I have 100 balls in the air and I'm trying to give each one the attention it needs. I'll concentrate on this one, or that one, or maybe I'll try to juggle two or three (and we all know my experience with balls is limited). It feels like I'm driving a car on a road built for normal cars but mine's not normal. It looks okay from the outside, but on the inside it's a bit rickety and I know there's something fucked up about it. My car doesn't work like the other cars, but I have to try to keep this car on the road that's designed for normal cars.

Now that I know why I am the way I am, I am trying to come up with ways to manage it. I want to figure out how I can function better and achieve more. I've got better at controlling my outbursts, though the people close to me still cop it at times. I feel the pressure building inside me till it explodes out. I can say hurtful things, behave like a child, and afterwards I feel absolutely awful. I remember having this sense of shame and remorse as a child, too. I'd feel absolutely shit about myself because I knew my behaviour was out of line. I have certainly damaged relationships along the way, I know I have. I've had to rebuild relationships, and there have been others that haven't been easily fixable.

I have so much gratitude for my parents. They never shamed me or made me feel bad. My mum is the most patient human in the whole world. I am hugely grateful for Mum's love. She loves me unconditionally, and as I've got older I've realised how lucky I am to have her, because not everyone has a mum like mine. She's never been adversarial, confrontational or competitive. She is accepting, non-judgemental and so incredibly patient and kind. And Mum knows me so well as a person. She knows I have explosions, but that I'll come back around and I'll apologise and that deep down I'm not a totally shit human.

Sophia, too, has come to understand why I don't handle things as well as I should sometimes. It must be hard for her, though, when I'm so locked in a negative pattern of thinking and there's no pulling me out of it. She has to sit by and wait till I can get myself back on an even keel. Sophia knows now that all she can do is put on my favourite animation film, *Ratatouille*, and make me a cup of tea. It's not lost on me how lucky I am to have found someone like her.

* * *

Something that *has* changed is the way I talk to myself now. Getting the diagnosis has led me to be kinder to myself and to view my flaws in a more compassionate light. Having ADHD means going through life hearing far more negative thoughts — both from others and from yourself — than neurotypical people. We're told we're too much, we're not enough . . . and over time how can that not affect your self esteem and how you are perceived in the world? Now I'm aware of this, I am letting myself drop the self-blaming. I know now that my brain is wired a little differently and my anxiety and sense of overwhelm isn't because I'm flawed. It's just part of who I am.

There are lots of things that come with ADHD that I am really proud of and grateful for. Like the fact I come alive when I'm on-air. The giant dopamine hit that comes with live broadcasting means that hosting radio is what I do best — I can think on my feet and be spontaneous. I have learnt that my ADHD brain thrives in pressure environments. It's about the only time in life where I find my thinking feels clear. And my ADHD is responsible for my creativity, which I think is probably my biggest super-power. I have always been creative — coming up with imaginative ideas seems to come naturally to me. In fact I find it effortless and fun, and when I'm being creative I'm at my happiest.

I believe ADHD makes me more sensitive, too. And I mean that in a good way. One of my skills in life is being able to help others; and because I feel things deeply, I feel like I know how others are feeling. I am the person my friends come to when the chips are down, or if they're anxious or depressed or in a pickle. I've talked so many people out of panic attacks and scary moments. Maybe because I've been there myself many times over, I never find it hard to know what to say. I genuinely feel that when the people I love are hurting, I hurt too — and all I want to do is help them feel better.

Two little mice

You know that Steven Spielberg film *Catch Me If You Can*? There's a scene where Frank Snr, the dad of the con-artist main character, gives a speech about two little mice who fell into a bucket of cream. The first mouse quickly gave up and drowned. But the second mouse wouldn't quit. He struggled so hard that eventually he churned that cream into butter, and was able to crawl out.

Working in media sometimes feels a bit like that. It is such a competitive industry that every single person who has a job knows there are a hundred others queuing at the door for an opportunity, so you have to work your little arse off to make sure you keep yours. It can feel like you're part of a giant chess game. Entire television stations are closing down, journalists are out of work everywhere you look, and even though radio is still doing alright, it is impossible not to feel insecure. People are moved between roles with little warning or choice and restructures loom on every horizon.

Even though I've never lost a job in my life, being an anxious person means I'm still kept awake at night by the fear of not working in the industry I love. The tenuousness of the job, that lack of job security, works away at my soul and there are times when the stress gets to me. I reckon everyone who works in the radio industry feels it . . . that edginess, that little bit of anxiety knowing you won't be flavour of the month forever.

Because of all this, my MO from the very start of my career has been to say yes to pretty much every opportunity that comes my way. This could all end tomorrow, so I might as well pack as much as I can into it while I can. Moving to New Zealand was one of those 'say yes' times. And so was auditioning for *Celebrity Treasure Island*.

While some people use a radio job as a stepping stone into a television career, I had only ever considered myself a radio person. I'd never thought of myself as a contender for a TV role, perhaps because growing up I didn't see anyone on the telly who looked or sounded remotely like me. Aussie TV stars were beautiful, slim, blonde and very polished. They looked like they all came from the same factory, which was definitely a different factory to the one *I* came from! Their factory was much more Sydney than Stanthorpe.

But in 2019, Dean, my boss at ZM, told me he'd been approached to see if I might consider being a contestant on *Celebrity Treasure Island*. The beloved Kiwi reality show was being rebooted after a long hiatus. It would involve two teams of seven celebrities, all dropped off on a desert island. They would compete in challenges that would either win them clues to a $100,000 prize to donate to their chosen charity or lose them players, as celebs would be eliminated each episode. I was flattered to be asked and I loved the idea of competing, but there was one major issue. I wasn't a celebrity. I'd only been in New Zealand for a year; no one would have known who the hell I was.

'Good point,' said Dean when I reminded him I wasn't famous.

Then he asked if I would be interested in auditioning for a hosting role on the show instead. Of course I thought, 'Sure, why not?' There was absolutely no way in hell I thought I would get the job, as I'd never done any television whatsoever, but I was always up for a new experience.

'Okay, I'll see if I can get you an audition.'

Next day, Dean told me he'd scored me a 'pity audition'. This, he explained, meant the auditions had closed but the producers had agreed to let me have a go as a bit of a favour. There was no suggestion that I was in the running but they were happy to give me some experience with an audition in front of a bunch of Warner Bros production people — the ones in charge of making the show.

Of course, because I am the least chill person on the planet, I flew into a big, fat stress attack. What the hell was I thinking?! I'd never done any TV in my life, how would I know what to do? I wasn't good enough for telly! I read over the script I'd been sent and it just didn't sound right. The gags weren't the kind of things I'd say and it didn't sound like the language I'd use. So, without really thinking, I grabbed a pen and re-wrote parts to suit me better. It was a risky move, but this was a pity audition so it didn't really matter, did it?

On the morning of the audition, I was beside myself with nerves. The only thing keeping me on an even keel was the fact I'd be doing it alongside Matt Chisholm — the seasoned TV presenter who had already been selected to host *Celebrity Treasure Island*. Matt had fronted *Survivor NZ* a year earlier and I bloody loved him on that show. There was something about him I adored; he didn't feel like your typical TV presenter. He was authentic, raw and real. And this cobber had some good banter too.

I kept telling myself the audition was just for experience and didn't really matter, but of course I wanted to impress. The weird thing is, the moment I walked into the studio and saw Matt, I relaxed. He somehow managed to put me at ease. It sounds weird, but from the first moment I met him I felt like I'd known him my whole life. Maybe it's because we're both a pair of country kids who've somehow landed in this crazy world of broadcasting and still can't quite believe it.

As soon as the cameras were rolling and the audition began, a sense of calm washed over me. It was the same feeling I have when I'm on radio. The nerves disappeared and I came alive, somehow effortlessly throwing banter back and forwards with Matt as though it were the most natural thing in the world. It was fun. I was energised. And Matt was so supportive and welcoming, and he laughed at every one of my gags. He was generous with his laughter, which is such a nice trait.

I am usually hard on myself. I usually think I haven't done as well as I should have, or that I could have prepared more or said things differently. But this time I walked out of that audition feeling great. I was on a high, and rang Dean as I skipped out of the studio in Grey Lynn and headed to my car. 'I know it was just a pity audition and nothing's going to come of it, but I fucking nailed it!' I told him with a huge smile on my face.

Two weeks later, Dean came to see me at work. 'Guess what?' he asked. 'They've offered you the gig.'

Excuse me?

'They've offered you the hosting role on *Celebrity Treasure Island*. They loved your audition and think you and Matt will be a great team.'

Oh my god — was this for real? I was shocked and happy, but before I knew it my old mate anxiety had popped back. The negative voices were coming in hot. 'You?! TV?! You can't do this! You're not good enough for telly! You'll never be able to learn the lines. No one even knows who you are. What if everyone hates you? What if it's a total flop?'

I wish I had been able to celebrate this amazing step in my career, but my anxiety and fear were making the whole business quite unpleasant. I doubted myself. And I didn't want to embarrass myself. I didn't want to fall on my arse while the cameras were rolling. I didn't want everything to go tits up and leave me with no choice but to go back to Australia and never show my face in New Zealand again.

I called Matt. 'I'm freaking out,' I said. 'I don't think I can do this job. I'm not right for it.'

Matt is my fucking hero, because he has had his fair share of mental-health battles in his time and he knew exactly how I was feeling. 'I've got your back, Bree. You're going to be great.' He told me to take my worries about not looking and sounding right and turn them into positive thoughts. Imagine how good it would be for kids at home to see people like us hosting a big show like *Treasure Island*, he said. 'They'll be able to look at you, a kid from the country, a rough-around-the-edges tomboy, and see that anyone can make it.'

In that moment I really believed Matt had my back. I knew he would support me. And he always has.

That didn't mean I wasn't a complete wreck by the time we flew out to Fiji to film season one. The night before I was due to leave, Sophia came over to my place to help me pack. At that stage we hadn't been together long so she hadn't found out yet what I was really like. But she got a rude awakening when she found me sobbing among piles of clothes and suitcases. 'I can't do this,' I said.

I am the worst packer in the world; I get completely overwhelmed. My ADHD brain was incapable of working out what I needed for the three-and-a-half weeks away. I was also trying to learn my lines for the first shoot-day — I had pages and pages of script spread out on my bed — and the task felt impossible. I was thinking, 'How will I ever remember all this off by heart?' I had never done anything like this before in my life. I had no idea what a TV shoot was going to be like and I was crippled with nerves.

I was also trying to learn all the contestants' names and their background stories, because despite this being 'Celebrity' *Treasure Island*, this Aussie import hadn't heard of any of them.

'I don't want to go. I can't go. I'm not going.' I was in full meltdown mode. Sophia was probably thinking, 'Oh shit, this girl has problems . . . what have I signed myself up for?'

Somehow, Sophia got me through the night without my mental state escalating. She helped me pack, made sure I had my passport and my toothbrush, and after a tearful goodbye I made it on to the plane. I felt like a fish out of water. Everyone else seemed to know each other but I was Nigel No-Mates On Tour. We took a bus from the airport in Nadi to our hotel down the coast and I sat alone for the whole of the five-hour trip, quietly losing my mind over what was to come. When we arrived, I went to find Matt. I needed someone to help me get on top of my anxiety.

I was obsessed with learning the script to the point that it was making me crazy. 'I'm so worried I won't be able to learn these lines and I'm going to fail,' I said to Matt. 'I'm struggling to hold it together.'

'Mate, me too. Should we sit down and go through it together?'

Matt and I walked back to my hotel room and sat outside

on the balcony that looked over a little marina and the ocean beyond. We went over our lines together. I began to calm down. Matt had done so much TV before, and even he was nervous. Just knowing that helped so much.

* * *

The first two days were set aside for media interviews and promotional photo shoots. I was shocked to learn that while hair and make-up artists were provided for contestants, the budget didn't cover hair and make-up for me. Shit! I would have to work out how to make myself presentable for TV. I had no idea where to start. The Fijian humidity didn't help either — my hair was standing on end like I'd been electrocuted. Throughout the three-and-a-half weeks of filming, I spent an hour straightening it each morning, yet the minute I walked outside it went 'poof!' and blew up like a giant fluffy poodle. I was so sweaty that by the end of each day I had mascara running down my face and most days looked like a drowned rat floating down the River Thames. My SULA (sweaty upper lip alert) became a major problem. I was so ugly I was worried we'd be losing viewers. (Fortunately the bosses learned from their mistakes, because hair and makeup was provided for me in subsequent seasons.)

As the first day of filming got closer, I was still struggling with this business of learning the script. I went to talk to our producer, Tim Lawry (or Long Story, as he's fondly known, because he bloody loves telling a long story). He's a lovely guy, but when I asked him how closely I needed to follow the script, he looked a little concerned. 'Um, yeah, it's best if you stick to what's there on the page.'

Aha! He didn't say I HAD to stick to it word for word. That was good enough for me. I decided I would do what I'm best at — which is ad-libbing. I would make shit up as I went along, just like on the radio. For the first episode, the introductory one, I made sure I followed the script when it came to explaining the rules to contestants. But all the other stuff — well, I made it up on the spot. And the more creative I was, the more I came alive. Matt was doing the same and we both felt things were going great. We were bouncing off each other and having fun.

At the end of the first day, Long Story approached me. 'Uh oh,' I thought. 'This could be bad.'

'So, Bree . . . we didn't really stick to the script, did we?'

I was in the shit, I knew it. 'Um . . . no, sorry about that Tim.'

He smiled. 'I loved it! Keep doing it,' he said. Then he asked if it was true that this was my first time in front of TV cameras. 'Well, you'd never have guessed it,' he said. 'You were fantastic.'

The relief! He was so supportive and he liked my style. It was just the confidence boost I needed. After that, my anxiety settled and I realised that TV wasn't all that different to radio — it was about being authentic, creative and open. Rather than trying to be a TV presenter, whatever that meant, I just had to be myself.

People always ask me what it's like behind the scenes on

Celebrity Treasure Island, and if what's shown on TV is what it's really like. I can say, hand on my heart, that what you see on TV is exactly what it's like on set. I reckon the key to the success of the show is that the stars are pushed to their absolute limits and forced so far out of their comfort zones. Just because they're 'famous', they're not getting any special treatment. They really are left out in the wild. They're sleeping rough, living on beans and rice and getting attacked by bugs and insects. There's no secret food truck that rolls in after dark, and no luxury hotel rooms out of sight. They're washing in the sea and sharing one disgusting portaloo which absolutely stinks.

Luckily for the hosts, we get to stay in a hotel down the road.

When it comes to storylines, there's very little interference from producers. Having said that, every reality TV show has a story producer whose job it is to ensure we're making good television. They don't dictate the overall storyline, but they might make suggestions to contestants on strategy, or perhaps encourage them to talk to another person about an alliance or whatever. But because there are such big sums of money involved, with the contestants all wanting to win for their chosen charities, the rules around how much they can get involved are really strict. Producers can guide people in certain directions, but the challenges are left to play out completely on their own.

In the final *Celebrity Treasure Island* challenge in 2021, where Chris Parker, Lance Savali and Edna Swart were digging for the $100,000 treasure, the producers thought it would take about 20 minutes before we got a winner. Matt and I hid in a

TWO LITTLE MICE

bush to watch the action unfold. We had to be quiet, because our mics were on, and ready to jump into the shot as soon as the treasure was found to be like 'Congratulations, you just won *Celebrity Treasure Island!*'

The problem is, neither Matt or I are very patient. An hour passed and then two, and we were starting to get pretty bored. Out of nowhere, Matt produced the world's biggest fart. It sounded like a cannon going off. He looked as shocked as me. Shit, it was funny. We were cracking up so bad but trying to stifle our laughs so we didn't get in trouble and muck up the finale. Matt and I had a long-running 'who can fart loudest on mic' competition, but this was a clear winner. I stored that moment away, and when we were back in Auckland I asked the audio girl to dig it out. I played Matt's fart on the radio and it still makes me laugh thinking about it. Matt wasn't the only one to suffer humiliation, though. I pissed my pants during a shoot on the beach and spent the rest of the day's filming hoping people wouldn't notice the wet patch on my tan-coloured shorts. Another time I got stung by a bumblebee in my armpit and had to ignore the fact it was swelling up like a balloon as the cameras were rolling. I was thinking, 'Great, I'm going to die on camera.'

The beautiful thing that I have really come to appreciate about working on *Celebrity Treasure Island* is the bonds and friendships that are formed. Everyone arrives on set feeling worried and alone, but by the end the relationships are quite special. I mean, I'm only the host and I feel forever bonded to some of the people I meet on the show, so I can't imagine how much more pronounced that would be for the contestants who go through hell together. It's always such a diverse bunch of people, and that's meant I've connected with some surprising people. In season one, Jodie Rimmer and I really hit it off. She's totally off the wall and seemed to get my jokes; she would laugh so hard I bloody loved it. Dame Susan Devoy is another *Treasure Island* bestie and I just adore her. She might be abrasive on the outside, but on the inside she's the softest, squishiest teddy bear. Matty McLean was an unforgettable contestant because he was such a die-hard fan of the show. It was his dream to take part, and when he didn't win I thought the tears would never end. Six seasons of *Treasure Island* later, I have never met anyone as desperate to win as Matty. Thank god he took out the top spot when he went back to compete in *Fans v Faves*.

Day one of filming is always the scariest for me, because I feel really vulnerable standing up in front of all those celebrity contestants — many of whom are far more experienced TV people than me. Imposter syndrome sets in and I can't help but think, 'You'd be so much better at this than me.' I'm thinking I'm not good enough to be there and it takes a lot for me to push through those initial wobbles. I'd love to say that I feel totally confident in the role now, six seasons in, but that would be a big fat lie. I still have a full-blown panic attack every time I agree to do another season, those negative voices in my head wondering why they've asked me back and telling me I'll do a bad job this time.

I watched a clip on Instagram recently where an expert

talked about the effect of ADHD on self-esteem. He said that despite how far people with ADHD get, no matter how much they achieve or how successful they are, the self-confidence battle never ends. The sense of not being good enough lingers. That really resonated with me because I am constantly second-guessing myself. But deep down, somewhere inside me, I must have some inner self-belief because I keep putting myself up for these jobs. Either that, or I'm a masochist. Pressure makes diamonds, right? Though I'd say I'm more of a cubic zirconia — fake it till you make it!

I don't know what it says about me that I actively choose roles that are raw and revealing — there's nowhere to hide when you're on radio and TV. I have realised I keep saying yes because I know that once it's all over, I will look back and finally allow myself to feel proud of what I achieved. With every season, I tell myself I can't do it and I'm going to be a flop, yet then I surprise myself. Hosting *Treasure Island* is one of those accomplishments where it hasn't felt easy or come super-naturally, but shit it feels good when you've pushed yourself and you achieve something you can be really proud of.

I loved working with Matt because our chemistry came so naturally. We worked well together, almost like we were meant to come together on that show. We were talkers and we were both sensitive, so we connected on a deep level, and I just thought it was so brave the way he was open about his mental health. It's hard to admit when you're struggling, but Matt knew he could help others by being honest. And I was so impressed by his strength.

He had all the similar struggles with lack of confidence as me, but then I'd see him being amazing at his job. He has a special way of talking to people and building instant connections. I felt really lucky to have him by my side on *Celebrity Treasure Island*.

I never would have imagined our duo would end. But it did, because after season three Matt wasn't asked back. Matt has talked publicly about his devastation, writing in his book that he believes the problems started in season three, when we had a new person join the *Celebrity Treasure Island* team. Right from the start, we all had to adjust to a new way of doing things, which wasn't necessarily easy in the high-paced, pressurised environment of the shoot. It was a really tough time. An unexpected Covid lockdown had added an extra week to the schedule, and I know Matt hated being away from his family and his routines. Plus we were all reeling from the death of one of our contestants, Va'aiga Tuigamala, just days after we arrived on set. It was devastating, I cried for two days straight. So yes, there were lots of things that made season three a tough one, and there were moments during filming when things felt strained. But in the end we all went home feeling like we'd managed to create a great season and we had plenty of fun and hilarious times along the way. I don't think anyone who was involved would ever have imagined that Matt wouldn't be asked back.

I was gutted to lose Matt, and I was scared about doing *CTI* without him. I suppose I could have had a big old tantrum and walked off the job in protest, but I never considered it. I have been in the media industry long enough to know that bosses make decisions for all sorts of reasons, and part of being an adult is learning to roll with the punches. You're never going to agree with every move or every change — I certainly didn't think that getting rid of Matt was the right choice, but I had to suck it up and embrace what came next. And luckily, working with my new co-host Jayden Daniels was fun. Our rapport and chemistry was different to what I'd shared with Matt, of course it was, but we got on great. It was the same with season six, when Lance Savali, a previous contestant, joined me. I loved working with him, he's such a sweet guy.

Losing Matt as a co-host meant I had to be brave and stand on my own two feet. I couldn't rely on him to hold my hand anymore. That made me nervous to start with, but I realised that after three seasons I had learned a lot and I actually knew what I was doing. I started to believe in myself more.

* * *

A big confidence boost came in 2022, when I was nominated for TV Personality of the Year at the New Zealand Television Awards. I didn't think I had a hope in hell of winning, though. I was up against broadcasting legends like Mike McRoberts, Paddy Gower and Nadia Lim, so I knew my chances were slim. I mean, I'd only done three seasons of *Celebrity Treasure Island* by that time — I was a total novice compared with those stars.

But I did have one thing going for me, and that was my

community of 1.5 million lovely people who follow me on social media. The Television Personality of the Year award is the only award of the night that is decided by public vote, so even though I felt embarrassed, I thought 'Fuck it, I'll ask for help.' I would never usually ask the people who follow me for anything, but I swallowed my pride and asked for a minute of their time to vote for me. And it just went ballistic. The response was amazing. I had thousands of messages from people saying they'd voted and wishing me luck.

Still, when the big night rolled around I didn't think it would be me who took the prize. I'd never won an award in my life; why would this be any different? Maybe that's why I ignored my manager's advice to go easy on the booze until after the award was announced. With my friend Cam as my date because Sophia was working, we were in the mood for a party so we hit the free drinks hard.

I was dolled up to the nines in a sheer black skirt and jacket situation and had my hair and make-up done. I was having a great time, and had almost forgotten I was nominated by the time my friend Kim Crossman got up on the stage and started talking about the Personality of the Year Award, which she was presenting. She started saying really nice things about someone — and the things she was saying felt kind of familiar. 'Hold on, is she talking about me?' I whispered to Cam. Oh *shit*, she's talking about me!

'And the winner of the Television Personality of the Year Award is — Bree Tomasel!'

WTF? I won!!! Cam was screaming in the seat next to me, telling me to get up and go to the stage. I had not — of course — prepared an acceptance speech and I was definitely not what you'd call sober. But I was bloody delighted, and as I climbed the stairs to the stage to accept my award I had a very clear moment of being so incredibly thankful for where I'd found myself. To think that those Warner Bros and TVNZ people had taken a chance on this unknown Aussie who'd never done TV in her life just blew my mind. And as for the amazing community of people who like what I do on social media, this would not have happened if they hadn't voted for me and supported me. I still have moments where I can't believe so many people like my weird videos and enjoy my humour, but I have worked my arse off to create this special little community and I'm proud of it. Mostly, I couldn't believe I was up there, accepting this award. I thanked everyone I could think of and skipped back to my seat where I proceeded to celebrate in a big way. It really was one of the most exciting and happy nights of my life. It still gives me goosebumps when I think about that award and that's because it was voted on by the public. That made it feel so much more special than if it had been chosen by a bunch of old pale and stales.

I love to think that me being up there might have shown people that anyone who has enough drive and determination can make it in television. You don't have to be super-polished, or look and talk a certain way; I am proof that there actually is room for people like me who don't fit into the usual female-on-TV mould. I really hope that any kids at home who might feel a bit weird or different can see that you don't have to be perfect, or well put together, or completely confident — you can be a bit rough around the edges and vulnerable and still do pretty bloody well on TV.

Whitney Houston and Meryl Streep

Although Mum has never talked to me about her own trauma from the home invasion all those years ago, I know she was scared because soon after it all happened, she and Dad decided we needed a dog. And Bella wasn't just any dog — she was a 65-kg bull mastiff–wolfhound cross whose enormous size and ridiculously deep bark made her perfect for the job of making me and Mum feel safe again.

Bella came from one of Dad's workers who'd got her as a pigging dog, but it turned out she wasn't much into pigs so he offered her to us. From the moment I laid eyes on that giant hound, it was love at first sight. I adored her and she adored me.

I would lie down on the ground next to her, snuggling in for a spooning session, Bella's paws draped over the top of me, and I felt safer there than anywhere. I was doing my best to put what happened out of my mind, but for a long time I couldn't shake the feeling that those guys would be back. Having Bella didn't magically make the fear disappear, but I knew that if those arseholes *did* turn up they'd have to deal with her first. And I knew she would have torn them to pieces before she let them near us.

Every family should have a dog, right? There's nothing better than that wagging tail and happy face that meets you at the door after a hard day. If you're feeling shitty or down, a dog instantly makes you feel better. They don't nag, they don't sulk, and they don't come at you with passive-aggressive undertones. They give you all the unconditional love you could ever need. And in the case of my two pooches, Whitney Houston and Meryl Streep, they're so insane they make me laugh my head off every day. But it's more than that. I have always felt an incredibly deep connection with animals. Often they can calm me in a way that a humans aren't able to. The unconditional love you can share with a dog is incomparable, there's nothing else like it.

Sophia and I got our first dog, Whitney Houston, after we'd been together for a couple of years. We both knew we wanted a dog but we couldn't work out what breed to get. Fluffy or short-haired? Big or small? Puppy or old dog? Rescue or purebred? We *umm*ed and *ahh*ed and walked around parks staring at other people's dogs, trying to work out what would be best for us.

WHITNEY HOUSTON AND MERYL STREEP

On one of those dog-stalking walks we met a cute little pooch that looked just like Toto from *The Wizard of Oz*. This dog was adorable. He had short little legs, a cute smiley face, pointy ears, and an energy that really spoke to us. He was bounding around the place, looking like he wouldn't be scared of anything, and I remember thinking 'That is a cool little dog.' The owner told us it was a Cairn terrier, so from then on we were fixated on getting one for ourselves. We even named our Cairn terrier before we'd found her: Whitney Houston.

'Why?' you might ask. What do you mean, 'Why'? Whitney Houston is the mother of all mothers, as us gays say. She's an absolute icon and if anyone deserves honouring in this way, it's her. And when we finally found our future dog on Trade Me — a teensy, tiny, teddy-bear fluff-ball of a puppy — the name could not have suited her better. She is unhinged (in a great way), has an excellent vocal range and can be a bit of a diva. She's also not super-keen on bathtubs. Bad taste? Too much? I apologise.

And amazingly, we discovered that our Whitney has the exact same birthday as the real Whitney Houston. August 9. Is that not the most batshit-crazy coincidence you've ever heard? I am convinced the spirit of the real Whitney lives on inside our four-year-old Cairn terrier.

Dog ownership was a little more work than Sophia and I had anticipated, especially as it turned out that Whitney was an absolute maniac of a puppy. For the first three months she was a psycho, there's no two ways about it. We couldn't walk through the room without her coming for us, leaping from the sofa on to our feet and latching her mouth around an ankle, sinking her teeth in. She chewed through shoes and electrical cords, and even our bed got torn apart. She pretty much terrorised us 24/7. 'Why does our dog hate us?' we'd ask each other. We loved her so much, yet our love did nothing to calm this psycho ball of fluff down.

Over time, though, she got better and we began to realise just how clever she was. We've put heaps of time into teaching her tricks. She can sit, lie down, play dead — all you have to do is point a finger-gun at her, yell 'bang, bang' and down she goes, legs in the air . . . she's a genius! Whitney is still bat-shit crazy, but that's why we love her. I look at other people's dogs being all normal and think, 'You're so boring.'

Whitney was so out of the box that when we had her spayed, she developed what's called a phantom pregnancy, where her body thought she was pregnant. The vet told us he'd never seen it in his twenty-year career. The poor girl was miserable — her nipples filled up with milk but because the puppies existed only in her mind, all that milk had nowhere to go. She ended up getting quite sick with mastitis. Sophia and I googled it and found that chilled cabbage leaves are the thing for humans with this miserable condition, so that's what we did — we bought a cabbage and laid the leaves on our dog's engorged nipples, sitting up with her all night for a week trying to make her feel better. If people had looked in the window and seen what we were up to — tending our dog with huge swollen boobs covered in chilled cabbage leaves — they'd have thought we were fucking crazy. And you know what? Maybe we were.

It gets weirder, though, because one night soon after the operation I carried Whitney down to the lawn in the dark for a wee. She couldn't take herself because we were scared her stitches would rip out. Anyway, she was drugged up and drowsy and it was taking her forever to do her business. I, too, was suddenly busting for a wee. 'Hurry up, please Whitney,' I whispered. But it was no good. I couldn't leave her on the lawn by herself, so instead I whipped off my PJ bottoms and squatted down next to her. Mum, who was staying, happened to come outside right at that moment to find her daughter pissing like a dog in the front yard. 'Oh, Brianna! What the hell are you doing?'

But honestly, I loved Whitney so much that being caught weeing on the lawn was a small price to pay for what she brought to my life. Sophia and I were besotted, and Whitney became the classic first-born child. She had all our time, attention and energy, and we would have done anything for her. But like most spoiled first-borns, this precious period didn't last. Two years later we went on a reality TV show to find ourselves a second child. *The Dog House NZ* was a matchmaking kind of situation where an animal charity paired prospective dog parents with pooches. Given how many dogs there are out there in need of homes, Sophia and I had decided that if we were getting another dog we would like to adopt. We felt bad that we hadn't done that with Whitney, but we lived and we learned.

The big day arrived and we turned up at the set of *The Dog House* excited to meet who we hoped would be the perfect brother or sister for Whitney. The puppy that had been chosen for us was cute, there's no denying that, but one look at his giant paws told me he was going to be *big*. No one knew what breed he was, but those twelve-week-old paws were bigger than Whitney's fully grown paws — they were almost the size of saucers. It was clear that he was going to be HUGE. I knew our house wasn't big enough for a giant pooch. I also knew we didn't have the time or skills to train a massive dog, either. While Sophia would have said yes straight away to avoid the awkwardness of turning down the dog on TV, I knew this plus-size pooch wasn't right for us.

After that we were taken to the dog charity headquarters and introduced to another potential pet. Out came Charlotte, a quiet, sweet precious little doggo with eyes so deep and soulful we could hardly look away. She was five months old, a lovely medium size, and so affectionate we knew we had to have her. No one knew what breed she was either, but we didn't care. She was perfect. 'This is the one,' Sophia said. And I knew it, too, but first we had to introduce her to Whitney. A lot was riding on this meeting. Luckily they got on like a house on fire, playing together in the yard like they were meant for each other. 'We'll take her!' we told the people. (We did end up doing a DNA test on her, and it turns out she's 50% Staffy, part American pitbull, part American bulldog, with a bit of Border collie. A bit of everything — a bitzer.)

Once we'd decided she was ours, it was time for a name. Charlotte's fine, but we wanted something a little punchier.

WHITNEY HOUSTON AND MERYL STREEP

Whitney Houston could not have a little sister with a boring name; it simply wouldn't do. I suggested Tina Turner, but Sophia wasn't convinced. 'Meryl Streep?' I asked. 'Perfect,' said Sophia.

Meryl is much more anxious than her ballsy big sister. She is needy, and if she had her way she'd be attached to a human at all times. At night she lies across me and Sophia on the couch, stretched out across us both and staring into our eyes. Being a rescue, it's like she can't quite believe her luck that we found each other. And we feel just the same. But because poor old Meryl is the second child, we never got around to teaching her any tricks at all. Compared with the attention heaped on her older sister, Meryl got shit.

She also managed to give us shit once, after eating every single chilli off the plant in our garden. We didn't realise what she'd been snacking on till I got home one afternoon to what I can only describe as a poo-nami. The entire house was coated in dog diarrhoea — she'd sprayed the red-hot liquid on to every imaginable surface. Walls. Beds. Couch. Carpet. Even the ceiling didn't escape.

I forgave her though because Meryl is my ride or die. She's my emotional support dog. She's my go-to if I'm having a rough time. There have been many, many times when Meryl is the only thing that can calm me down when I'm in the midst of a panic attack. Sophia will take one look at me and know what I need. 'Hang on, I'll go get Meryl!' She'll plonk her down next to me, tuck us both in with a blanket, Meryl's soft little head resting on my shoulder and her eyes looking up at me with all the compassion you could ever need. It's like she has an intuition and an understanding of what I'm going through. She's the cuddliest, sweetest and most sensitive dog in the world.

***

Despite the initial meeting where we thought Whitney and Meryl were instant BFFs, actually they hated each other for the first few months. They fought every day, biting and growling and wrestling on the floor, making me and Sophia stressed out and upset. After one particularly nasty bust-up over food, which left Whitney with a bleeding paw, we knew it couldn't go on. 'If it happens again, we'll have to choose one to re-home,' we agreed.

Those dogs must have heard us, because that was the last fight they ever had. After that, Meryl assumed the submissive position and Whitney took control. Like in all good relationships, they just had to figure out who wore the pants.

Menty-B #2

A big factor in my decision to move to New Zealand was the knowledge that I was only ever a three-hour flight away from my family. Yes, I'd be living across the ditch, but I could jump on a plane home if I needed to or Mum and Dad could come to me. And at the start it was great — we visited each other loads. Mum would visit every few months, and I went home at least three or four times a year so the distance didn't feel any harder than when I was on the Central Coast.

But then Covid-19 hit and everything turned to shit. A global pandemic wasn't something any of us could have anticipated. Being trapped in a country away from my family for almost two years wasn't a situation I saw coming. And for an asthmatic like me and someone with a history of health anxiety, the threat of this deadly virus was pretty fucking scary.

The first lockdown was kind of fun in an 'all in it together' kind of way but that nail-in-the-coffin Auckland lockdown in 2021 — the one that lasted for months and months — nearly finished me off. As the weeks turned into months, my anxiety worsened and I was beginning to feel seriously low. I was consumed with missing my parents, because I knew I would never have moved to New Zealand if I'd known what was coming. Being unable to see my family was a nightmare and missing two Christmases with them left me feeling so lost.

Life was weird. Every day I'd drive into the city on a deserted motorway, find a park right outside work, and enter the eerie building that used to be a hive of activity and now felt more like an abandoned office block. So much of what Clint and I chat about on-air is inspired by our normal, everyday lives. But nothing funny was happening to anybody anywhere, and none of us were doing anything at all other than being stuck in our stupid homes, so drumming up content became really bloody hard. Yet at the same time, we knew people needed us. They needed the laughs, the escapism and the company more than ever before. So we worked hard, doing everything we could to come up with ideas to keep people entertained and sane during that time. We came up with stupid games like Quarantine Cluedo where we'd ask people to call in from their houses. Then we could ask them two questions with the aim of guessing which room they were in. 'Is the room you're in carpeted?' Or, 'Would you have sexy times in this room?'

I know what you're thinking: award-winning radio it was

MENTY-B #2

not. But times were grim and we were grasping at straws.

On the face of it, I probably looked okay. I had Sophia, thank god, and our relationship was the best thing in my life at that time. But the distance between me and my family felt wrong and scary. I was surrounded by Kiwis who I don't think could quite understand what I — and many other people — were going through. Don't get me wrong: I know others had way worse situations, like family members dying alone in hospital. But stories like those were weighing on my mind and starting to send me into a downward spiral.

I thought it was only a matter of time before things went badly wrong — and my parents wouldn't be able to get to me. Or I couldn't get to them. What if Mum or Dad got sick? What if they got Covid and died before I could say goodbye? What if *I* got sick? would I have to die alone without my family by my side? Totally dramatic, yes, but these things were actually happening to other people and I couldn't shake the anxiety, which was growing by the day.

For too long, I kept my fears to myself. Every night I lay awake, fearing the worst. New Zealand's zero-Covid strategy was keeping the virus out, but I knew what was happening around the world where the pandemic was totally out of control. And I couldn't see a time when the borders would ever open again. The uncertainty about when I might get to see Mum and Dad again was literally driving me crazy. Before long I was locked in a constant state of anxiety. My heart raced as though I was being chased by a knife-wielding robber. I was exhausted, stressed and my body felt like it had absolutely nothing left to give. But even though I'd been through this before, I ignored the warning signs. 'I'm okay, I'm okay, I'm okay,' I chanted as I slowly but surely lost control of my mind.

It was during this never-ending lockdown that I woke one morning to find my arm was numb. You know that feeling, right? When your arm's gone dead because you've been lying on it in a funny position? That's all it was, but because I was on the verge of a mental breakdown I had lost the power of rational thinking. I went into panic mode. My health anxiety took over and life tumbled into complete disarray. 'What's happening with me? This is the end.'

Questions and fears about my health flew around my head constantly. I knew I was losing the plot. I guess I even knew, deep down, that I probably wasn't dying, but once again I felt trapped inside my own mind. I was a prisoner to these thoughts, I couldn't get away from them, and it was absolutely fucking terrifying. Maybe because I'd had a mental breakdown before, I knew how bad things were going to get.

I'm great at helping others when they're struggling, but when it comes to dealing with myself, when *I* start losing it, I'm hopeless. I don't have the tools to work my way out of it. I have absolutely no idea how to help myself, and that's a horrible feeling. From that day when I woke with the numb arm, I shut off from everyone, including Sophia. I didn't want to talk about the feelings I was having because saying them out loud made me even more anxious.

MENTY-B #2

I had convinced myself I was getting multiple sclerosis. I thought about it constantly. Watching TV, walking the dogs . . . whatever I was doing, my mind was on my health. I'd be inventing symptoms and feelings in my body to confirm my suspicions that I was in a bad way. I was completely exhausted. I felt as though I had no control whatsoever over my brain. In that heightened state, I was so convinced there was something wrong in my body. I was on high alert for any tweak or twinge that would further confirm my belief that I was sick and dying. 'I'm fucked,' I'd tell myself. 'I'm fucked and my parents won't even be able to get here to help me.' The anxiety was there 24/7, even when I was on-air each afternoon. Continuing to work when I was in that state was the hardest thing I've ever done in my life, and I look back now and wonder how the hell I did it.

And just like the last time, I started to have actual physical symptoms. My brain was fucking with me to the point where my hands felt numb and my body shook. I felt so flawed and vulnerable and broken, but I didn't know how to let Sophia help me. I'm still amazed she stuck by me after that. She's seen me at my lowest, that's for sure.

But even in my darkest moments I was always determined to fight to get better. I knew I needed help, so I dragged myself to the doctor. I begged her to give me something, anything, to help me get some control back. 'I feel like a zombie,' I told her. I had always rejected antidepressants in the past. I don't know why, but I'm scared of taking meds. This time felt serious, though, and I agreed I would try. I began taking sertraline, a drug for treating depression and anxiety. Anyone who's been on antidepressants can tell you that finding the right one can be a process. I knew this, and I was warned about side effects, but nothing could have prepared me for how sick I felt. The pills made everything ten times worse. I was so nauseous I gave up eating — I was already off my food thanks to the crippling anxiety, but this was next-level. Even thinking about food made me want to vomit. I lost 11 kg in a month.

The worst part, though, was that I started to experience a side effect called brain zaps, which felt like electric shocks to the brain. The internet told me these were usually experienced by people when they were coming *off* antidepressants, but for me these painful zaps, which felt like a shooting pain right through one side of my head to the other, lasted the entire four months I stayed on the drug. I stuck it out because the doctor had told me it would take a while to settle.

I saw a therapist during this time, too, recommended to me by someone. The first couple of appointments went okay. I told him what had been going on, I explained how Covid and the stress of being away from my family had sparked my health anxiety, and I told him I didn't think I could take much more. It takes a lot for me to talk openly about this stuff, but I was determined to give this a good shot so I really opened up. On about the third or fourth appointment, though, we were discussing the health anxiety and I mentioned I was terrified of Google, because researching symptoms on the internet in the past had led me to some very dark places.

MENTY-B #2

'Let's confront that fear right now then, shall we?' he asked.

'No, please no. Please don't do this.' I didn't want to find out what could be the cause of my numb hands and shaking body — I wasn't strong enough to know what it was I might have.

But the therapist picked up his phone and started typing my symptoms into Google. I couldn't believe he was doing it. I had tears streaming down my face and was begging him to stop. But he persisted, reading out the various conditions that could be related to my physical complaints. Despite the panic attack that was happening right in front of him, he kept going. I couldn't take it. I stood up and walked out, never to return.

He messaged to check in on me a few weeks later, and I never messaged him back. I wish I had, though. What I should have said was, 'What you did in that room was traumatic for me, the worst possible thing. I told you "please don't do that" yet you kept going.' Thinking about it now still makes my blood boil. I paid *$320 an hour* for that fucking idiot!

I was so miserable. The brain zaps were terrifying and only made my anxiety more horrible. After three or four months, I made the decision to stop taking the drugs. I felt like I was finally seeing light at the end of the menty-b tunnel — the clouds were beginning to part — and I knew the antidepressants weren't serving me. From the moment I came off them, I felt a massive wave of relief wash over me. I started to feel like me again, and over the coming weeks things got easier. The crisis was over.

When the travel restrictions were finally lifted, I got on one of the first planes out of Auckland and flew to Brisbane.

Eighteen months without a hug from Mum had been the hardest thing I'd ever faced, and our reunion was amazing. I surprised them: travelling for ten hours and turning up in Stanthorpe unannounced. Walking into the lounge and asking, 'What's for dinner?' They stared at me like a couple of stunned mullets. Then we cried, hugged and laughed and I knew everything was going to be alright.

***

I had kept my first mental breakdown a secret. I didn't want anyone to know what had happened to me because I was embarrassed and ashamed. Back then, I felt like I was the only one who couldn't cope with life. This time, though, I decided. I needed to be honest. I wanted to be transparent with my audience because I knew that so many others were in the same boat. The real pandemic, I felt, was the mental-health crisis the lockdowns had created. I decided I didn't want to be someone who doesn't share the real side of life. Part of me thought that if I shared this on radio, it might make me feel less alone — and maybe, just maybe, it might make others who were struggling feel a little less isolated, too.

I told Clint before we went on-air that I was going to talk about my anxiety. He wasn't certain it was the right decision. 'Are you sure you're up to this? Are you sure it won't upset you?'

I think he was worried I might fall apart on-air. But I was adamant. I knew it was time for me to be honest about my mental health. I was ready to talk about this super-raw, super-intimate detail about my life. And unusually for me there would be no funny ending, no punchline, and no big laugh at the end.

My heart was racing as I began to speak. 'In the midst of one of the craziest times our generation will probably ever go through, I wanted to ask people listening out there, are you okay? And if your answer is no, that's okay. Because I feel the same.

'Right now I don't feel okay. And it doesn't mean we're weird, it doesn't mean we're different. It just means we're being honest.'

As the words tumbled out of my mouth, I knew it was the right thing to do. I knew other people out there were struggling and I wanted them to know they weren't alone.

After the show, the clip of me talking about my mental health went up on our ZM Facebook page and people seemed to notice it. My inbox was filling up with hundreds and hundreds of messages. It could have been thousands of messages. It was completely overwhelming how many others were going through awful things — it was clear there were so many people feeling the same way I was. And everyone was thanking me for being brave enough to talk about it.

One message stopped me in my tracks: 'Hi there, I'm not normally the type of person to message radio hosts or people in the media, but I was in the car today, and I was on my way to do something to myself. I thought I just couldn't go on anymore. All of a sudden you came on the radio and you started talking about what was going on with you. In that moment, your voice telling me how you were struggling in this world made me feel less alone. I turned my car around and went home.'

A message like that is a very stark and moving reminder that the connections I make with listeners can be so meaningful. It was a reminder that while we spend most of our time making people laugh and acting like larrikins, we can also make a difference. That message will stay with me forever, and it's the reason I will continue to be open about the hard stuff. I am willing to brave whatever storm comes my way because I have got to the point where I feel like this is my purpose — I am privileged enough to have a platform where I can use my voice to be real and authentic. So often social media portrays life as a highlights reel, but it's important to acknowledge that life can also be difficult and hard to navigate at times. I hope I represent people who might not see or hear someone they relate to in everyday mainstream media.

I have never regretted anything I have shared and I am so pleased I made the decision not to hide my sexuality when I moved to New Zealand. I didn't subject my listeners to a giant coming-out event, because why the hell should I? Instead I just talked about my dating life and relationships with women as openly as my straight co-hosts did, without batting an eyelid.

Back in Australia, hiding such an important part of who I was meant there was a distance between me and my listeners, even if I didn't realise it at the time. That double life ate away at my soul. Now though, I'm free to be who I am. And I know that being open about being queer — as well as about my mental health — has resonated with listeners. I get messages all the time from young people who are still trying to figure out who they are and where they fit.

One boy, he was probably about fifteen, messaged me looking for support and answers about the way he was feeling. 'I've never said this out loud to anyone before,' he wrote. He was so sweet and so lost. We chatted. I could sense the toll all the secrets and shame were having on him. It broke my heart, and I tried my best to tell him he was normal and great and there was nothing wrong with him. I provided an ear where he could say what he was feeling out loud and I was able to reassure him that everything would be okay. I love the idea that I can be a safe space for people.

I'd also love to say that all our listeners react positively to my openness, but of course there are always a few trolls lurking in the murky canals of judgement and bigotry. Sometimes it's simply a 'Wait, what? Is Bree dating a girl?' type question, which is fine, I guess. Other times the comments are downright nasty. The one I'll never forget went like this: 'I didn't realise Bree was one of those people who flaunts her bisexuality, or whatever it is she says she is. She's setting a bad example for my twelve-year-old daughter and we are turning off your show and we won't listen again.'

The idea that I was a bad example to his daughter hurt like hell. I felt like I'd been punched right in the gut. Taking my headphones off, I stood up out of my chair and walked out of the studio. I needed five minutes to compose myself, so I headed to the bathroom, sat down on the toilet, and cried. Usually I'm able to laugh off nasty comments, but this one stung. I am a good person — I know that. Why does the fact that I love a woman mean I'm a bad role model?

When I walked back in, I saw that producer Ellie (my friend who helped me get my ADHD diagnosis) had called the number and was talking to the man who'd sent the message. I only caught the end of the conversation but I could see she was fuming. 'Bree is an amazing person and we don't need listeners like you,' she said, slamming the phone down on the desk. Her loyalty meant the world to me.

Trolls are all part of being in the public eye, and most of the time I have a pretty thick skin. But there are some who leave their mark. My least favourite troll first reared her ugly head during my second season of *Celebrity Treasure Island*. Her name was Karen, I kid you not. Or Kween Kockhead Karen, as I came to name her. KKK made it her life's work to let me know just how shit I was at my job. Every time a *Celebrity Treasure Island* clip was shared on social media, there she was telling everyone I was a terrible TV host and should never have got the job. Under every story about the show Karen would appear, commenting about how useless I was and how much she hated everything about me. According to Karen, I should go back to Australia because my voice was terrible and I was fat and ugly.

Most importantly, though, KKK wanted everyone to know I was NOT funny at all. And if anyone stood up for me, she'd get stuck into them too. She really fucking hated me. And after a few weeks of this, with her comments popping up on every possible platform, it felt like a relentless hate campaign. She even started tagging me in mean posts. I'd love to say it didn't affect me, but it did. I was angry at this mole of a human and I couldn't understand how someone could be so full of hate towards a person they had never met. What did I do to her? Nothing, that's what!

This story has a happy ending, though, because (of course) not all Karens are part of the Kockhead Kingdom. Around the same time all this was going on, I got a friend request on Facebook from a random Karen. I thought it was KKK coming for me, so I accepted and got ready for a good old brawl. But — no such thing. We got chatting, and this Karen was of the nicest women I've ever met; she could not have been more different from KKK. We became firm friends, and I learned that she was facing incurable breast cancer. Suddenly the shit KKK was throwing around faded into nothing. It was a great perspective check. Lovely Karen was so inspiring in the way she faced her disease with positivity and courage. I ended up doing a charity walk with Dame Susan Devoy in support of this amazing woman.

I reckon this is the perfect example of turning lemons into lemonade. Ghastly KKK led me to the best Karen you could ever know and a friendship I'm so grateful for.

The Great Sperm Hunt

Halfway through my thirties, it is finally time to accept that I am an adult. I've done my best to dodge and dive adulthood for long enough, but growing up simply can't be avoided any longer.

If it were left up to me, I would be a poor excuse for an adult. But Sophia has helped me. She swooped in, her Super-Grown-up cape billowing out behind her, tied me up by my ankles and dragged me (kicking and screaming) into adulthood. We got our two dogs, Meryl and Whitney. We bought a house. We have a GIANT mortgage. We pay bills, we save for new carpet, and we talk about kitchen renovations that we'll never be able to afford. There is no escaping it — we have hit peak adulthood.

THE GREAT SPERM HUNT

And being adults means we've found ourselves thinking about having a baby. We want to be mums! Sophia and I have always talked about starting a family together, but until now it's been an 'in the future' type thing. Something that feels faraway and wistful. But now we can't ignore the fact that our biological clocks are ticking. Mine more loudly than Sophia's, thanks to my chequered history of 'women's troubles'.

Sorry to state the obvious, but there's a quite major hurdle when it comes to us and baby-making. Sophia and I only have half the necessary ingredients; there's no chance of a 'happy accident'. So instead of romance and sex, we have a shit-ton of decisions to make and logistics to consider. Which one of us will carry a baby? How do we find someone to give us sperm? Where do we even start?

Unsurprisingly, the process of becoming parents for same-sex couples makes me feel overwhelmed. Sophia, of course, is calmer and she's confident we can do this. She gets the ball rolling by booking us an appointment to talk to a doctor at a fertility clinic. I want to be a mum, I do, but I'm also scared. I am full of doubts and fears, the most pressing one being that my body won't be up to the task and will fail at the first hurdle.

Driving to the appointment, I feel sick with nerves. I'm not good with doctors at the best of times, but I can't shake this awful feeling that I am about to find out that my problems are going to ruin this for both of us. I have a bad feeling the doctor was going to take one look at me and say, 'Nope, not gonna happen with this one.'

We take the lift up to the third floor and sit down in the waiting room with the other nervous-looking women and handful of men. We do what the others are doing, scrolling on our phones and flipping through magazines but this — nor the soft music and calming neutral décor — does nothing to help my nerves. 'Why are you freaking out?' whispers Sophia. 'It's just an appointment.'

We follow the doctor into her little consulting room and tell her we would like to have a baby together. She is lovely. She tells us she has helped lots of same-sex couples become parents. Then she explains how the process usually works. There are two options in terms of sourcing sperm — we could go on the two-year waiting list for an anonymous donor, or we could try to find a 'personal donor', someone we know who would be prepared to help us. We would need to decide which of us wanted to carry a baby and whose eggs to use. And we would all need to go through counselling to make sure we were mentally prepared for the long process ahead.

The doctor talks us through IVF, the process of joining our eggs with donor sperm to create embryos. She tells us the cost — around $20,000 for each round — and once we've recovered from *that* little shock, she asks us about our reproductive health. Have either of you been pregnant before? No. Have you had any issues with your cycle or reproductive health? No, said Sophia, before handing to me.

This is what I've been dreading. I am a repeat offender when it comes to women's troubles.

***

At age twenty I was diagnosed with polycystic ovary syndrome (PCOS), a hormonal disorder that causes a whole bunch of symptoms, including weight gain, irregular periods, cysts on the ovaries, and facial hair (the one symptom I thankfully avoided — a miracle given that I'm also half Italian!). Other than horrifically painful periods throughout my teens, my main problem was the onset of terrible skin. I woke up one day covered in pimples and I bloody hated it. Mum obviously realised that my pizza face was something to do with my hormones and since my sister had been diagnosed with PCOS, she thought I should get checked out too. She took me to a gynaecologist, where an ultrasound showed that, like Amber, I too had cysts on my ovaries. I was put on a strong contraceptive pill to try to fix the hormonal imbalance. My skin cleared up almost overnight, so I was delighted, and I didn't give much thought to what those polycystic ovaries might mean for my fertility further down the track. Who's thinking about babies at twenty? Not me, that's for sure.

A year after the diagnosis, though, I started to get stabbing pains on the left side of my abdomen. I couldn't work out what the hell was causing it. The pain wasn't period pain; I knew what *that* felt like. This was much sharper, would strike at any time of the month, and was so severe I'd have to stay home in bed, clutching a hot water bottle to my tummy.

Mum took me back to the gynaecologist, who suspected

endometriosis, a condition where tissue grows outside the uterus. Endo causes all sorts of problems: pain, bad periods — and infertility. Only an operation would tell me how bad it was, though. I woke up from the general anaesthetic feeling sore and disoriented. I had no idea what they'd found, or how bad things were, until the surgeon popped into my room three hours later. He explained that he'd made an incision through my belly button and found significant endometriosis on my left side, which would account for the pain I'd been having. He had also cut into me near my hip and found endo there, too. 'We've scraped it off all the places it shouldn't have been,' he said, cheerily.

Jesus, it sounded bad, though part of me was relieved they'd found something and the pain hadn't been in my head. But I hated being in hospital and just wanted to get out of there. After one night I was sent home, where Mum took care of me at my flat for the next week.

Who knew that constipation can be a side effect of surgery and all the hardcore drugs you get given? I went six days without a poo and things were getting desperate, so Mum went out to the pharmacy for laxatives. Thank god, I thought, gulping down two and waiting for action. After 20 minutes, nothing had happened — not even a stirring — so I took another two, ignoring the instructions which said the pills can take up to six hours to work. Oops, I'd double-dosed myself. I tell you, what happened that night was like the Chamber of Secrets. I took off like a rocket on the toilet with Mum listening outside the door cheering me on.

I'm amazed I got my bond back on the rental property because I fucking destroyed that shitter.

I digress.

One of the things the specialist warned me about after the surgery was that endometriosis can affect fertility. Obviously, at 21 having babies was far from my mind, but fast forward ten or so years to that fertility doctor's office with Sophia, and those words were coming back to haunt me. Was it going to be me who let the side down?

I told the doctor that while my endometriosis pain was helped initially by the surgery, it returned after a year or so and had never really gone away since. The pain has continued throughout my life to the point where I feel it every day. Some days it's a 1 out of 10 and that's a great day. Other days it's a 7, or it might be a 10 — that's when it feels like someone has a knife and they're dragging it up and down my uterus.

One of the worst times was when we were filming season two of *Celebrity Treasure Island*. I was run down, exhausted and the pain was almost unbearable, but I had no choice but to continue. Amazingly, the legend that is Candy Lane was a contestant, and her chosen charity was Endometriosis New Zealand. She spoke about her daughter's battle with the condition and her resulting fertility problems, and I couldn't hold it together. I burst into tears while the cameras were rolling. I felt so grateful to Candy for shining a light on this fucking awful thing that so many women endure silently.

Over the years I have been to several specialists to try to get help for the pain. The last doctor I saw advised me to avoid more surgery until I'd had children, because further scraping could affect my fertility even more than the endo itself. 'The more we operate, the lower your fertility goes,' he said. 'If you're wanting a baby one day, the best chance you'll have is to hold off on surgery and deal with the pain.' So that's what I've done.

After downloading all that (bar the laxative explosion) on the fertility doctor, I nervously asked if she thought my issues would make it impossible for me to have a baby. 'Not at all,' she said, adding that we wouldn't know the full picture of my fertility until we'd done more tests. She also pointed out that despite the incredible advances in fertility medicine, there was still a lot of mystery. Sometimes people in perfectly good working order found themselves unable to get pregnant easily; and sometimes miracles occurred, with women falling pregnant against the odds. Coping with uncertainty has, of course, never been my strong point, but somehow I would have to accept these unknowns if we were to embark on this journey.

One of the first blood tests Sophia and I did was to assess our AMH levels, which would tell us what our egg stores were looking like. It was the first step in determining our fertility levels. Sophia's were pretty good, and mine were not so good. My biological clock was ticking very loudly, and we knew we didn't have the luxury to wait any longer. We needed to find our own donor and get cracking.

But is there anything weirder than drawing up a list of men you know (some well, and some not so well) and contemplating the suitability of their sperm? I don't think so. Yet the minute Sophia and I walked out of that appointment and got in the car, we couldn't help ourselves — our minds turned to all the guys we'd pretty much ever met and the contents of their ball sacks. It felt like we were standing at the supermarket pick 'n' mix selecting nuts. Would we go for the solid yet smooth macadamia? Or the outrageously expensive 'take out a second mortgage' pinenut? All we knew was we didn't want to end up with the most boring nut of all, the Brazil nut. Our sperm chats went something like this:

'What about Ben?'

'Ben who?'

'Ben Jones. You know, we met him at Bella's barbecue.'

'The good-looking blonde one?'

'Yeah, the hot guy who makes the casually racist jokes.'

'Ew, no thanks.'

'Yep, let's not risk a racist. How about Pete?'

'Pete! He'd be great! He's funny and he's nice but I doubt his wife would be keen on us milking her husband like a dairy cow.'

'Good point. Jeremy! Let's ask Jeremy!'

'Are you crazy? Jeremy's favourite TV show is *The Big Bang Theory*. He is not suitable to be the biological father of our hypothetical children.'

I am, of course, joking. For the first time in my life I didn't actually have many jokes to make about this little baby-making journey we were embarking on. It felt like the scariest yet the most important thing I'd ever done. It was also serving as a near-constant reminder that being in a same-sex relationship puts us squarely outside of 'normal' again. Sophia and I would love to keep our baby plans to ourselves. We would love to create a baby privately. Instead, for us to become mums we need doctors, nurses, genetic material from another person and shit-loads of money. Even a fifteen-minute appointment just to *talk* about having a baby costs $280.

When it came to looking for a sperm donor, there were several factors we weighed up. We liked the idea of whoever it might be resembling at least one of us even just a little bit. Also, because we're shallow, we liked the idea of someone who's at least vaguely decent-looking. We weren't hanging out for David Beckham; we're not *that* delusional. But someone above a 5 out of 10 might be nice.

Personality was important. They needed to be nice, funny and kind, and definitely couldn't be a weirdo — let's be honest, I bring enough dodgy genetics to the table already. Most importantly, we needed to find someone we could trust. There couldn't be a higher-stakes arrangement on the cards, so we would have to be absolutely certain we were all on the same page and were in it for the right reasons.

Personally, I think that being asked to share your sperm is one of the biggest compliments a guy could get. But the idea of actually asking someone to do this made my blood run cold. How fucking awkward. 'Oh hey, random man, can I ask you a favour? Would you mind wanking into a cup for me to shove up my foof and potentially create a baby who you won't get to raise?'

Sophia and I were often in stitches at the ridiculousness of the whole bloody business. It would have been a whole lot simpler if we were straight. I totally understand and acknowledge the many straight couples who go through hell trying to have a baby, but I do hope that those who find it easy — those heterosexual couples who can decide to have a baby, have sex, then hey presto we're parents — realise the immense privilege that is.

Gay men are often the first port of call for lesbians looking for sperm donors. There are various reasons for this — queer people are usually open-minded when it comes to families that look a little different to the mum plus dad plus kids norm. Or perhaps they're just great people who don't mind helping out a couple of lezzies here and there.

After going over the list of men in our lives who we thought might like to share their sperm, Sophia and I landed on our friend Josh. For some reason that we couldn't quite pinpoint, we thought he'd be an amazing donor. We first met Josh a few years before at our local dog park. He had posted on a community Facebook page asking if anyone with a puppy might like to meet up for a puppy playdate. We'd recently adopted our adorable-but-nutty Whitney Houston and thought some social interaction with another doggo would be good for her. Our first date with Josh went well — we hit it off and the dogs had a ball — so we started meeting up more regularly. Josh's partner Tom joined in too, and before we knew it us four were friends.

I promise you we didn't have eyes on Josh's sperm when we first met, but now that we were professional sperm-hunters we couldn't get him off our minds. He's a lovely, warm man. Tall, with olive skin and green eyes, and weirdly I think he looks a bit like me. He's in his early thirties and has a daughter who he had when he was very young after a brief relationship with a woman. The fact that he was a dad already was appealing. Not only did it mean his swimmers were proven to be effective, but we wondered if he'd be more open to the idea of giving us the greatest gift of all because he already knew how special parenthood was.

But how the hell do you ask someone out of the blue if they might be willing to share their sperm and help you have a baby? It's a huge thing to ask of someone; the very idea made me feel nauseous. And the situation was complicated further by the fact that Josh and Tom had recently moved away from Auckland. There wasn't going to be a chance meeting at the dog park where we could throw the old 'Want to give us some sperm?' question into the conversation.

We agonised over how best to approach Josh. Was a text message too casual? Would a phone call catch him off-guard? An email felt too formal. Fuck — should we revive MSN Messenger? Finally, we ended up composing a text:

'Hi Josh, hope you and Tom are well. I know this message will take you a bit off-guard but Bree and I are going down the path of trying to have a baby and your name came up as someone who might be able to help us as a donor. We were wondering if it's something you might consider. There is no hurry to respond to this, think it over for as long as you need, and please don't feel bad if it's not for you. Thanks for reading this. Bree and Sophia.'

THE GREAT SPERM HUNT

It sat on Sophia's phone for another few weeks before we finally got brave enough to press 'send'.

We did it! We sent it! Then we waited.

A few days later, Josh wrote back. 'Hi Bree and Sophia. Thanks for thinking of me. I will need to think this over and talk to Tom about it. I'll come back to you soon.'

Okay, well, he didn't say no, so hope was not lost.

A few weeks went by and we didn't hear anything. Obviously, being the fatalist I am, I told myself the silence meant Josh hated us for asking him in the first place and we would probably never hear from him again. But finally another message arrived, and it was Josh suggesting the four of us — me, Sophia, Josh and Tom — have a Zoom chat to talk it all over. The dream wasn't over after all!

And there was more to that message: he and Tom wanted to discuss a potential swap. Our text had got them thinking about the future, and they'd realised they'd like the option of having a baby together one day too. Perhaps we could come up with a kind of trade arrangement — swapping our eggs for their sperm?

Ooh. We hadn't even thought about this possibility, but Sophia and I talked about it and concluded that it would be only fair to consider it. It felt like trading Pokémon cards.

The Zoom call went well. I was surprised by how natural it felt to talk about such major life issues with Josh and Tom. We were all being honest with each other, and we all spoke about how the arrangement might work. Sophia and I had decided that in an ideal world, if everything went perfectly and to plan, our dream would be to each have a chance at carrying a baby. In this ideal world, I would be pregnant with a baby made with Sophia's egg, and she would carry a baby made with mine. We wouldn't be pregnant at the same time because, well, two newborns — no thanks. But that was the dream. Bree and Sophia with two little kids born a couple of years apart, living happily ever after just like a normal family. It almost felt greedy saying it out loud. Now, I'm terrified that by writing this motherhood fantasy down I might be jinxing it.

While nothing was finalised or promised in that Zoom chat, we all agreed to go away and continue thinking things over and regroup a few weeks later. In the meantime, Josh and Tom visited a fertility clinic and we went back to the doctor in Auckland to begin the process.

* * *

So far, so good, right?

Sure! It's exciting. But I'm finding it hard to block out all the negative thoughts whizzing around my anxious brain. There are so many 'what ifs' in this arrangement. What if Sophia and I go through IVF and neither of us manages to get up the duff? Would we still give our eggs to Josh and Tom? What if they got a baby out of this and we didn't? Could we cope with that? What if Josh's sperm wasn't high-enough quality for IVF? What if we only produced rotten eggs? We also had to address the awkward topic of who paid for which parts of the process.

THE GREAT SPERM HUNT

Then there were the questions around what happens if we were lucky enough to have a baby. What sort of involvement would Josh and Tom want with a child made from Josh's sperm? What involvement would we be prepared to accept? It was a minefield. But amongst all these complex layers, I felt hugely grateful to have these like-minded, good people taking these first steps on this amazing journey with us.

The rational part of my brain knows that same-sex couples are having babies all the time and nailing all these complex issues. But I can't help but feel overwhelmed, though. Sophia is confident, of course. She wants to be a mum and we both know she'll be amazing at it. Me? I am riddled with doubts. Will I be any good at this? Will my body work properly? And if it does, will I be a good mum? Is it okay for a child to have two mums? Will it make life harder for our child? What if he or she gets teased for having two mums? What will people think? Will my parents be proud of me?

The shame, the shame, the shame . . . will it always be part of me?

I realise there are things I haven't dealt with internally to make me accept that I am worthy of having kids. There is a battle raging inside me, and accepting that I deserve to be a mum is the huge last piece in the puzzle to accepting myself for who I am.

Because Sophia doesn't have the shit-ton of anxious, obsessive, negative thoughts marching around her body, she is more confident than me. And thank goodness she is, because I know that one day in the future, if we are lucky enough to pull this off and become mums, it will be because she led the charge.

'Of course we can do this,' she says. 'You'll be amazing. You deserve this just as much as the next person.'

Sophia knows more about babies than most people do. She works days, nights, weekends with them at the hospital. She tends sick babies, premature babies, keeping alive these tiny little things who, for whatever reason, have ended up in her care. She lifts them out of their incubators and onto their parents' chests. She changes their nappies, bathes them, feeds them. She knows loss, too; she sees it every week. And when it comes to the idea of our own baby, that scares her. But it doesn't put her off. She wants a baby.

And so do I. I want this so badly. I want it for me, I want this for us, but I want it for Sophia even more. She will be an amazing mum. Sophia tells me I need to be brave and push aside whatever is making me so scared of this process. She reminds me how much I love kids. I do — I can't keep away from them. I want babies and I want to be a mum.

I tell myself, 'I am worthy of this.'

To be continued...

Here is a little story about coming out. I had just broken up with my girlfriend and moved into a flat with my brother Aden. I love Aden. He's easy-going, funny and a real sensitive soul, and this was the first proper time we'd spent together since I left home for boarding school. Aden was twelve when I moved out, but now he was 25 and I loved living with him. He didn't yet know I was into girls but lately I'd been seeing someone new called Bianca and I liked her.

Aden and I were driving to Woolworths to do the weekly shop when I blurted out: 'Do you mind if Bianca comes over for dinner tonight?'

'Yeah, that's all good,' he said.

'Um, you know, like, we're actually dating . . .' I said, my palms sweating and heart racing.

'Yeah, I know,' he said. 'That's cool. It doesn't change anything.'

It was like I'd told him we needed to get milk or bread. To Aden, my sexuality was the least big deal in the world. There was no sharp intake of breath, no surprised look on his face, no drama and no further questions. I didn't even have to tell him to keep his mouth shut about it to the rest of the family. He'd grown up in the same house as I did, so he just knew where I was coming from with Dad. But for Aden, it was nothing. It pretty much felt like how I imagine it would feel for heterosexual people when you say you're seeing someone of the opposite sex. Experiencing this was the nicest feeling in the world.

So, readers, be like Aden. If someone you love tells you they're queer, make sure they know it's okay. Make sure they know you still love them and that their sexuality doesn't change a thing. And be cool — no one needs a song and a dance and a parade through town. Yeah we do love a party, but not in this situation.

When I made Mum promise never to tell Dad about my sexuality, I had no idea the damage it would cause. Secrets, I have learned, breed shame. And shame, I have also learned, is hard to shake. If you're reading this and you're gay, please tell people. You have NOTHING to be ashamed of. If there's going to be an explosion, deal with that explosion now. I promise you that dealing with the hard shit early will mean you can be free. I would do anything to go back in time and be honest with Dad — I could have avoided ten years of anguish.

Please be proud of who you are. You are great! You are wonderful! You deserve to be yourself.

TO BE CONTINUED . . .

If you're reading this book as the parent of a child you know or think is gay, please talk to them! Don't be scared. Your child is the same person they were before you found out about their sexuality. Don't assume that they know you still love them. *Tell* them. Say the words. Please love them. Love them harder, if you can, because that child — no matter their age — is confused and scared and they need you.

I wish Dad had talked to me sooner. I'm not angry at him anymore because I know he needed time to work through his religious and cultural baggage and figure out how to accept me for me. I wish he'd been brave enough to talk to me about it earlier, and I wish I'd been brave enough just to tell him. I wish I'd found the courage because I know now it would have been okay. I didn't need to be so scared.

I know Dad thought I was doing fine. I would turn up back in Stanthorpe as loud and brash as ever. I probably looked happy. But I was hiding a huge part of myself and underneath I was sad and ashamed. I felt like I was less of a person than Amber and Aden, whose latest boyfriends and girlfriends were welcomed and embraced. Mum has told me that agreeing to keep my secret is her biggest regret in life.

Every queer person has their own story. And I am incredibly lucky compared with lots of people because I have my parents in my life who accept me and I am living authentically. And despite my anxious little mind, I am mostly really happy.

* * *

I didn't hear the term PTSD till much later in my life, but I am pretty convinced it's what I've been dealing with since the home invasion, when those scumbags turned my happy little life upside down. I don't have a formal diagnosis, but do I need one to know that what happened to me at age nine put my life on a different course? I don't think so.

I mentioned my PTSD self-diagnosis once to a psychologist, telling him I believed my lifelong anxiety was sparked by those two men who had burst into my nan's house. I told him that before that knife was pressed up against my neck, I was calmer, lighter and happier. I hadn't even considered that bad things could happen. Those bastards awakened a fear in me that has never really gone away. And when anything remotely scary happens now — by scary I mean worrying, stressful, hard, surprising — my emotional response is one of terror. My heart rate goes up, my palms sweat and I want to run.

The psychologist brushed it off. 'Possibly, but not necessarily.'

I know he's a doctor and smarter than me about these things. But I also know that at the heart of my anxiety is a fear of death. I don't think I need an expert to confirm where it started. Medications, I have realised, don't work so well for me. So now that I'm a fully fledged adult, I'm learning how to do things that help keep me mentally well. Exercise, sleep, good food, not too much booze — you know the drill, all the boring-but-good-for-you stuff. I am also trying to accept that sometimes my brain is a wild animal and I can't always control it. This wild animal has

TO BE CONTINUED . . .

its own agenda at times. I am an anxious person and I probably (read: definitely) always will be. But I surround myself with good people and I focus every day on the wonderful parts of my life, because the good absolutely outweighs the bad.

If you're feeling down right now, remember you are not alone. There are other people feeling like this, too. It's not your fault. Your brain is playing tricks on you. Hang on in there because some day soon those clouds will part and you will feel better. Turn to the people you know have your back. For me, it's Sophia and it's Mum. Mumma Di is the biggest influence in my life. She is the star of my world. Her love and support is unwavering and constant and I honestly don't know how I'd survive without that. She listens to ZM every day, agrees to be on-air whenever I ask her and lets me drag her into the most ridiculous antics on TikTok. I'm lobbying for her and Dad to move to New Zealand. I can't imagine Dad ever leaving Stanthorpe, but dreams are free.

If someone had told that awkward Aussie teenager twenty years ago that she'd be where I was now — settled and happy in New Zealand, working on a top-rating national radio show and fronting a hit reality TV show with a social media following of almost 1.5 million — she'd have thought they were crazy.

And if anyone had told Young Bree that Grown-up Bree would be living happily with a woman, planning babies with her, and talking freely about who she was on-air and in life, I'm not sure I would have believed them. The idea of Dad accepting and loving me for who I am felt like a faraway dream throughout most of my life. But he does. He loves Sophia, too. And I know that if we are lucky enough to make this baby dream a reality one day, he will be the best Nonno ever.

The biggest lesson I've learned is that real success didn't come to me until I'd found the courage to truly accept who I was and be completely and utterly myself.

Before then, there were roadblocks. I would think, 'What am I doing wrong?' I realise now that what I was doing wrong was holding parts of myself back. When I found the courage to be myself, *that's* when things fell into place. My social-media community grew to what it is today, an amazing community of funny, supportive and kind people, the radio show really started humming, and I finally began to feel like I belonged in front of the *Celebrity Treasure Island* cameras. If you'd told little gay me that I would be living happily and openly with a woman I love, with two crazy dogs and plans for babies under way, and that my whole family love and support us, I don't think I would have believed you.

But there we have it, folks — I am proof that things can work out even if you're weird, awkward and slow to bloom. Keep on going. You'll get there, I promise.

Acknowledgements

First and foremost, I want to thank my patient and selfless parents. I know I have taken you on a roller coaster that seems like it'll never end (spoiler: it won't) but your unconditional love, support and guidance has never wavered. I have heard people say that you're a reflection of your parents, and I hope this is true because if I end up becoming half the person that you both are I'll be able to hold my head high. Mum, the engine room and heart of our family, I wish you could see yourself how I see you. You are strong, funny, patient and my most favourite person. Thank you for being my biggest supporter, you accept me at my best but also at my worst and for that I will be forever indebted to you. Dad, salt of the earth, smart and witty. Thank you for showing me what true grit and determination looks like. A true come-from-nothing success story, your passion for your work, to provide for your family, your moustache and booming laugh will be your legacy.

My sister and brother, Amber and Aden. Sorry for the broken bones growing up but not sorry for the amazing memories we have created along the way. I am blessed to have such amazing siblings who I know would run headfirst into a knife fight with me if I asked them.

Sophia, thank you for wiping my many tears throughout the process of writing this book. For being the voice of reason (even when I wouldn't listen). You are my calm amongst the storm, my ride or die, and the person I love the most.

To the rest of my friends and family who have been named, thank you for being a part of my journey. Without knowing it you have shaped and impacted the person I am today. To those who weren't named, you got lucky this time haha.

Michelle Hurley from Allen & Unwin, thank you for believing I had a story to tell, even when I assured you I didn't. Your guidance and belief in me haven't gone unnoticed and I will be forever grateful for the opportunity to share my story.

The rest of the Allen & Unwin team — especially Leonie Freeman, Teresa McIntyre and Rebecca Simpson — thank you for your mollycoddling, sharing your expert experience and polishing this book until it was shiny and bright.

Dean Buchanan, my manager, mentor and friend. Without you I don't think this book would have ever been a reality. Thank you for backing me from the start, pushing me past my thoughts of doubt and having the biggest unwavering belief in what I'm truly capable of.

ACKNOWLEDGEMENTS

Lastly to my new lifelong friend, Sophie Neville. Who spent hours listening to my random drivel, translated my tears, anxiety and sporadic stories to create this book. A story that I hope will give someone the courage to live authentically as themselves. I am truly grateful for your incredible talent, openness to learn about the queer community, your sometimes needed brutal honesty and the amazing friendship you have shown me throughout this challenging process. I also want to acknowledge the passing of your beautiful mum — Pam Neville, who took a holiday to the clouds during this journey, she would be so incredibly proud of the person you are. PS. Let me know how much I owe you in counselling fees.

Well, that's it folks, that's literally all she wrote. Never in a million years did I think I would end up here, writing acknowledgements for a book. I feel humbled by this experience and opportunity. This process has been rewarding, cathartic and challenging. But through it all the goal has never changed, if my words and lived experience has helped and resonated with just one of you then above everything else it has been worth it. So I'll leave you with this: don't be defined by other people's definitions of you; define yourself. Be you, be free.